54.031

1857 IN INDIA

Mutiny or War of Independence?

PROBLEMS IN ASIAN CIVILIZATIONS

UNDER THE EDITORIAL DIRECTION OF THE COMMITTEE ON ORIENTAL
STUDIES, COLUMBIA UNIVERSITY.

EDITORIAL COMMITTEE: *Wm. Theodore de Bary,* COLUMBIA UNIVERSITY •
Ainslie T. Embree, COLUMBIA UNIVERSITY • *John Meskill,* BARNARD COLLEGE
• *Johanna M. Menzel,* VASSAR COLLEGE

WANG AN-SHIH—PRACTICAL REFORMER? *Edited by John Meskill*

THE CHINESE CIVIL SERVICE—CAREER OPEN TO TALENT? *Edited by Johanna M. Menzel*

DEMOCRACY IN MODERN JAPAN—GROUNDWORK OR FACADE? *Edited by George O. Totten*

JAPAN 1931–1945—MILITARISM, FASCISM, JAPANISM? *Edited by Ivan Morris*

1857 IN INDIA—MUTINY OR WAR OF INDEPENDENCE? *Edited by Ainslee T. Embree*

Other volumes in preparation

PROBLEMS IN ASIAN CIVILIZATIONS

1857 IN INDIA

Mutiny or War of Independence?

EDITED WITH AN INTRODUCTION BY

Ainslie T. Embree

COLUMBIA UNIVERSITY

D. C. HEATH AND COMPANY · BOSTON

Table of Contents

v

PART THREE: REREADING THE EVIDENCE

PART FOUR: SUMMING UP

Introduction

THE most written-about event in Indian history is the uprising against British rule in 1857. The interest that the war engendered was partly because it was one of the last wars of its kind, where courage and endurance, rather than heavy weapons, played a preponderant part, where beleagured garrisons held out against great odds, and where walled cities were stormed in a manner that recalled the wars of the Middle Ages, not the great battles of the nineteenth century. Furthermore, although the war was on a small scale and short enough in duration to be easily understood, it was apparent that great issues were being decided. To the excitement of forced marches in pursuit of a fleeing enemy was added the drama of seeing Western man pitted against Orientals, race against race, Christianity against the resurgent religions of India. These aspects of the uprising led to a vast amount of descriptive writing, much of little interest either as literature or history, except as it evokes the spirit of the times. There is, however, another class of literature that is of great value to the student of modern India: this is the interpretative writing that analyzed the nature and causes of the events of 1857. Out of this search for causes came a controversy that continued for about twenty years after 1857 and then died down, but which was reopened in the twentieth century with the growth of Indian nationalism, and has in recent years produced a whole new literature on the uprising.

In its simplest form, the controversy has centered around the name that should be used to designate the uprising of 1857.

Should it be called "The Sepoy Mutiny of 1857"? To do so indicates acceptance of the opinion that it was the fruit of grievances, possibly fictitious but certainly keenly felt, of the Indian soldiers in the British army in India. Or should the events be referred to as "The First War of Independence," indicating that they were an outgrowth of a militant Indian nationalism that at this early period sought to overthrow the power of a hated invader? In between these polar positions, a wide variety of theories have been advanced to explain the origin of a struggle that, by any reading, threatened the continuance of British rule in India. Since the writers, whatever their final conclusions, all used much the same sources, the divergence of interpretations provides a fascinating study in historiography. Almost without exception, the writers have proclaimed their freedom from prejudice and their intention of treating their materials with objectivity, yet their biases are strikingly evident in both the selection of evidence and in the value judgments they apply to it.

Despite the controversy over the nature and causes of the uprising, a sketch can be given of the events of 1857 that would probably be generally accepted by all the interpreters. At the beginning of the year there were a number of indications that the sepoys in the Bengal Army, the most important of the three armies of the East India Company, were restless and dissatisfied. The rumor that the bullets being issued to the soldiers were greased with cows' and pigs' fat was only one of the many signs of danger. But although there had been a number of cases of soldiers disobeying orders, the actual outbreak of violence came on May 10 when the Indian soldiers of the regiments stationed at Meerut killed their British officers and marched to Delhi, thirty miles away. The insurgents captured the city without much difficulty and proclaimed the Mughal Emperor, a helpless old man of eighty-two, as their leader. After a lull of three weeks there were new outbreaks among the civilian population in the Gangetic plain, especially in the former kingdom of Oudh, and in Central India. Delhi was recaptured by the British in September, and the two great cities of Lucknow and Kanpur were recovered six months later. The last remaining pockets of resistance in Central India were overcome in July, 1858, and by the end of the year British control had been completely restored, with the leaders of the uprising either killed in battle or put to death after summary trials.

From the first, the question uppermost in men's minds was what had caused the outburst of violence. Assumptions about the nature of British rule in India were called in question, and, almost for the first time, the rulers were forced to examine their position. It was widely believed that the Indians did not care who ruled them as long as they were left free to follow their immemorial customs, and, moreover, it was assumed that the British were so patently superior to their predecessors in respect to justice and in the establishment of internal security that the people were grateful to them. The loyalty of the sepoys to their British officers was also a matter of faith, and however much the character of other Indians might be denigrated, exception was always made of the sepoy. All these assumptions, the stock in trade of early nineteenth-century accounts of India, were suddenly called in question when sepoys and civilians throughout North India began killing both military officers and government officials. If the old beliefs were to be retained, or if new ones were to replace them, it was necessary to explain the causes of the

violence that had threatened imperial power in India.

The explanation of the uprisings that tended to be accepted in official circles in Great Britain and, to a lesser extent, in India was that they were basically army mutinies. This interpretation was appealing, because aside from the facts that undoubtedly could be marshalled in its support, it permitted the continuance of the belief that British rule in India had not awakened any deep antagonism. If the uprisings were the product of grievances that could be assuaged by such measures as better discipline and more attention to the details of army life, there was no reason for examining the presuppositions that had been used to explain the nature of British power.

That this interpretation was unsatisfactory was soon made apparent to contemporary observers by the widespread unrest among the civilian population. The identification of the causes of this unrest, and the explication of its relationship to the army mutinies, led to the long controversy over the events of 1857. The discussion leads into the main stream of modern Indian history by raising in its most insistent form the question of Indian reaction to British rule. This question is obviously of central importance to any understanding of the nationalist movement or even of the responses of the Indian masses at any period to governmental pressures. Because sources for such study are few, the materials relating to 1857 have a special interest.

Prior to 1857 there had been much discussion as to whether or not the pressures brought to bear upon Indian society by the government of the East India Company and by unofficial agents of Western power were too great. During the governor-generalship of Lord William Bentinck for the first time these pressures took the form of legislative enactments aimed at bringing about change in social customs. The prohibition of *sati,* the practice of widows immolating themselves on their husbands' funeral pyres, was the most dramatic use of administrative power to alter a well-defined social pattern, but later measures, such as the Act of 1850, which made it possible for converts from Hinduism to another religion to inherit ancestral property, was probably more widely resented. Government activities of a quite different kind, such as the introduction of railways and telegraphs and the encouragement given to the use of English as the medium of instruction in the schools and colleges, also produced changes within the social fabric. Added to these actions in which the Government played the leading role was the preaching of missionaries who, since 1813, had been allowed free access to the territories under the East India Company's control. Critics had warned the authorities for years that social legislation and missionary activity were regarded by many Hindus and Muslims as evidence that the Government had mounted an offensive against the old religions. By such critics the violence of 1857 was seen as an outgrowth of fear and distrust engendered by innovations. The obvious lesson to be learned, they urged, was that all attempts to bring about social and religious change, whether by legislative action or religious persuasion, should cease.

Related to this analysis of events was one that placed particular emphasis on political reorganization as a factor productive of unrest. One by one the states of Indian rulers had succumbed to British power, and in the 1850's, Lord Dalhousie, one of the most energetic of all the Governors-General in bringing about administrative changes, had annexed a number of the states which had been allowed to exist on a quasi-independent basis. One reason given for this policy was the failure of the ruling family to produce an heir; another was persistent internal misrule. Dalhousie's critics alleged that his action had lost Britain the support of the ruling classes and had aroused the hostility of conservative elements in the population generally by his seeming intention to subvert the traditional social order.

To these charges of interference the advocates of social change replied that so far from attempting in a hasty fashion to bring about a transformation in the social structure, the Government had moved with a caution that was at best exemplary of the consideration felt for an alien culture and at worst betrayed an unwillingness to accept the responsibilities inherent in the possession of despotic political power. For men like Dalhousie, the presuppositions of nineteenth-century European liberalism indicated the need for the rationalization of the system of power relationships in India. The political anomaly of a paramount power permitting the continuance of badly governed congeries of states within the general pattern of the control forced upon India scarcely seemed to require proof. For those who accepted the evangelical imperatives of Christianity —and there were many such men in political life in England and in the Civil Service and Army in India—the British Government and people had failed to fulfil the obligation of spreading the knowledge of the Gospel. The Mutiny was seen by them as a warning sent by Providence to call men to more serious Christian endeavor. Alexander Duff, one of the most influential missionaries in the nineteenth century, spoke of the violence of 1857 as evidence that "God is visiting our people in this land in hot displeasure," and argued that the events of the war would "portray to men's senses the cruelties of heathenism, and proclaim aloud the necessity of the regenerating, humanising influences of the gospel of grace and salvation."

Both those who opposed the forces making for social change and those who advocated them tended to see clear evidence in the uprisings of a widespread and well-organized conspiracy. Some identified the old Muslim ruling class as the source of leadership; others pointed to the dispossessed Maratha chieftains of Central India, who had fought most vehemently against the British at the beginning of the nineteenth century, and among whose number had been princes deposed by Dalhousie. A few commentators saw the outbreak as the product of Russian intrigues aimed at overthrowing British control. Whether in fact there was anything that can reasonably be called a conspiracy has remained one of the disputed issues in regard to 1857. Some students of the period have stressed the spontaneous nature of the uprisings in many parts of North India in 1857, and have argued the lack of coordination among even the military leaders as evidence that there was no initial planning of any consequence.

Of all interpretations of the uprising, the one that has had the most influence is that which sees 1857 as the year when nationalist feelings, long suppressed by British occupation, flared into violence. For these writers, 1857 is the First War of Independence, the moment when the ground-swell of smoldering discontent and hatred found expression in a passionate movement led by patriotic men and women to restore national governments in India. Back of this interpretation is the desire to show that the nationalist movement that won freedom for India is not a product of the late nineteenth century, and, above all, that nationalism is not an ideology learned from the West, but that there was a living sense of India as a nation that existed long before the advent of later political movements. This view is categorically denied by almost all Western and many Indian historians, who assert that nationalism in any meaningful sense cannot be found in the struggles of 1857.

All these views, and combinations of them, are found in the selections given here from a wide variety of writers. Some of them were contemporaries; some participated in the events they describe; others have examined the ample materials on the uprising, bringing to them a remarkable diversity of opinions. The selections are given in roughly chronological order, rather than being grouped according to interpretation, so that in reading them one can trace the interplay of arguments and note the development of ideas. It will be seen that almost all of the ideas were discussed at the time of the events, and that a process of refinement and reinterpretation has gone on through the years right up to the present time. One significant feature of the earlier writings is that they are predominantly British in origin; in the later period, on the other hand, many of the writers are Indians. This indicates not only changing interests, but also the unwillingness of Indian writers in the nineteenth century to commit themselves on a subject that had explosive emotional and political implications. Whatever their origin, however, the materials included here provide sources for an understanding of a major historical event and, even more, of the complex reactions that have created both modern Indian historical writings and modern India itself.

[NOTE: Footnotes have generally been omitted from the selections that follow, except where needed to explain the text.]

The Conflict of Opinion

"It was alleged that, this being a mere military mutiny, all we had to do was to put it down. . . . Now, I humbly think that the question of whether it is a mere military mutiny is one of primary importance. Is it a military mutiny or is it a national revolt? . . . The decline and fall of empires are not affairs of greased cartridges. Such results are occasioned by adequate causes, and by the accumulation of adequate causes."

—BENJAMIN DISRAELI

"As regards the feelings of the great masses of the people towards the British Government, the most contradictory statements have been put forth. Here, as elsewhere, extremes will be found wrong. That there ever was anything like affection or loyal attachment, in any true sense of these terms, on the part of any considerable portion of the native population towards the British power, is what no one who really knows them could honestly aver."

—ALEXANDER DUFF

"We have been almost as much to blame for what has occurred as have the people. I have as yet neither seen nor heard anything to make me believe that any conspiracy existed beyond the army; and even in it, one can scarcely say there was a conspiracy. The cartridge question was to my mind, indubitably, the immediate cause of the revolt. But the army had for a long time been in an unsatisfactory state. It had long seen and felt its power. We had gone on, year by year, adding to its numbers, without adding to our European force."

—SIR JOHN LAWRENCE

". . . it was clear that a very serious peril was beginning to threaten the ascendancy of the Priesthood. They saw that a reformation . . . once commenced, would work its way in time through all the strata of society. They saw that, as new provinces were one after another brought under British rule, the new light must diffuse itself more and more, until there would scarcely be a place for Hindooism to lurk unmolested. And some at least, confounding cause and effect, began to argue that all this annexation and absorption was brought about for the express purpose of overthrowing the ancient faiths of the country, and establishing a new religion in their place."

—SIR JOHN KAYE

"Indeed I may go so far as to declare that many of the actors in the drama failed to realise to their dying day that the outbreak was not merely a mutiny which they had to combat, but a vast conspiracy, the threads of which were widely spread, and which owed its origin to the conviction that a Government which had, as the conspirators believed, betrayed its trust was no longer entitled to respect or allegiance."

—G. B. MALLESON

"When, taking the searching attitude of an historian, I began to scan that instructive and magnificent spectacle, I found to my great surprise the brilliance of a War of Independence shining in 'the mutiny of 1857.' The spirits of the dead seemed hallowed by martyrdom, and out of the heap of ashes appeared forth sparks of a fiery inspiration. I thought that my country-men will be most agreeably disappointed, even as I was, at this deep-buried spectacle in one of the most neglected corners of our history, if I could but show this to them by the light of research. So, I tried to do the same and am able to-day to present to my Indian readers this startling but faithful picture of the great events of 1857."

—V. D. SAVARKAR

"The theory here suggested is the continuity of the Mughal Empire down to the deposition of Bahadur Shah in 1858, as an effective source of political authority and as the suzerain *de jure* of the East India Company in the capacity of *Diwan* of Bengal. . . . Governors-general . . . assumed an attitude . . . which could appear in no other light than that of high treason; and the culmination was reached when Dalhousie and Canning attempted to tamper with the succession. From that time it was clear that the over-powerful vassal must be reduced. The army turned to its sovereign's alle-giance against its rebel officer. Hence if in 1857 there was any mutineer, it was the East India Company."

—F. W. BUCKLER

"The Mutiny was inevitable. No dependent nation can for ever reconcile itself to foreign domination. A despotic government must ultimately rule by the sword though it might be sheathed in velvet. In India the sword was apparently in the custody of the Sepoy Army. Between the sepoy and his foreign master there was no common tie of race, language, and religion."

—S. N. SEN

". . . we can hardly expect a national war of independence in India either in 1857 or at any time before it. For nationalism or patriotism, in the true sense, was conspicuous by its absence in India till a much later date. To regard the outbreak of 1857 as either national in character or a war for independence of India betrays a lack of true knowledge of the history of Indian people in the nineteenth century."

—R. C. MAJUMDAR

PART I: INTERPRETATION DURING THE CONFLICT

An Indian Explanation

THE AZIMGARH PROCLAMATION

After the outbreak of violence in 1857, proclamations were issued by many of the Indian leaders calling upon the people to support them against the British. These proclamations constitute a major source of evidence for the causes of the uprisings, and are among the few documents we have from the Indian, in contrast to the British, point of view. Since they were written for a clearly polemical purpose, they cannot be regarded as wholly reliable guides to the feelings of the people, but at least they indicate the arguments that the leaders believed would have an appeal. The proclamation quoted here was issued by the forces that seized Azimgarh, a garrison town sixty miles north of Benares in the summer of 1857. Its general argument, that the new government was deliberately destroying the traditional patterns of society, is common to almost all the published statements of those who took part in the war against the British. The translation is given as it was first published, with one or two minor changes.

25th. August, 1857.

IT IS well known to all, that in this age the people of Hindoostan, both Hindoos and Mohammedans, are being ruined under the tyranny and oppression of the infidel and treacherous English. It is therefore the bounden duty of all the wealthy people of India, especially of those who have any sort of connection with any of the Mohammedan royal families, and are considered the pastors and masters of their people, to stake their lives and property for the well being of the public. With the view of effecting this general good, several princes belonging to the royal family of Delhi, have dispersed themselves in the different parts of India, Iran, Turan, and Afghanistan, and have been long since taking measures to compass their favourite end; and it is to accomplish this charitable object that one of the aforesaid princes has, at the head of an army of Afghanistan, &c., made his appearance in India; and I, who am the grandson of Abul Muzuffer Serajuddin Bahadur Shah Ghazee, King of India, having in the course of circuit come here to extirpate the infidels residing in the eastern part of the country, and to liberate and protect the poor helpless people now groaning under their iron rule, have, by the aid of the *Majahdeens* [religious warriors], erected the standard of Mohammed, and persuaded the orthodox Hindoos who had been subject to my ancestors, and have been and are still accessories in the destruction of the English, to raise the standard of Mahavir.

Several of the Hindoo and Mussalman chiefs, who have long since quitted their homes for the preservation of their religion,

Printed as a Proclamation of Emperor Bahadur Shah in Charles Ball, *The History of the Indian Mutiny*. London: 1860, vol. II, pp. 630–632.

and have been trying their best to root out the English in India, have presented themselves to me, and taken part in the reigning Indian crusade, and it is more than probable that I shall very shortly receive succours from the West. Therefore, for the information of the public, the present *Ishtahar*, consisting of several sections, is put in circulation, and it is the imperative duty of all to take it into their careful consideration, and abide by it. Parties anxious to participate in the common cause, but having no means to provide for themselves, shall receive their daily subsistence from me; and be it known to all, that the ancient works, both of the Hindoos and the Mohammedans, the writings of the miracle-workers, and the calculations of the astrologers, pundits, and rammals, all agree in asserting that the English will no longer have any footing in India or elsewhere. Therefore it is incumbent on all to give up the hope of the continuation of the British sway, side with me, and deserve the consideration of the Badshahi, or imperial Government, by their individual exertion in promoting the common good, and thus attain their respective ends; otherwise if this golden opportunity slips away, they will have to repent of their folly, as it is very aptly said by a poet in two fine couplets, the drift whereof is "Never let a favourable opportunity slip, for in the field of opportunity you are to meet with the ball of fortune; but if you do not avail yourself of the opportunity that offers itself, you will have to bite your finger through grief."

No person, at the misrepresentation of the well-wishers of the British Government, ought to conclude from the present slight inconveniences usually attendant on revolutions, that similar inconveniences and troubles should continue when the Badshahi Government is established on a firm basis; and parties badly dealt with by any sepoy or plunderer, should come up and represent their grievances to me, and receive redress at my hands; and for whatever property they may lose in the reigning disorder, they will be recompensed from the public treasury when the Badshahi Government is well fixed.

Section I—Regarding Zemindars. It is evident, that the British Government in making zemindary settlements have imposed exorbitant *Jumas,* and have disgraced and ruined several zemindars, by putting up their estates to public auction for arrears of rent, in so much, that on the institution of a suit by a common Ryot, a maid servant, or a slave, the respectable zemindars are summoned into court, arrested, put in gaol and disgraced. In litigations regarding zemindaries, the immense value of stamps, and other unnecessary expenses of the civil courts, which are pregnant with all sorts of crooked dealings, and the practice of allowing a case to hang on for years, are all calculated to impoverish the litigants. Besides this, the coffers of the zemindars are annually taxed with subscription for schools, hospitals, roads, etc. Such extortions will have no manner of existence in the Badshahi Government; but, on the contrary, the *Jumas* will be light, the dignity and honour of the zemindars safe, and every zemindar will have absolute rule in his own zemindary . . .

Section II—Regarding Merchants. It is plain that the infidel and treacherous British Government have monopolized the trade of all the fine and valuable merchandise, such as indigo, cloth, and other articles of shipping, leaving only the trade of trifles to the people, and even in this they are not without their share of the profits, which they secure by means of customs and stamp fees, &c. in money suits, so that the people have merely a trade in name. Besides this, the profits of the traders are taxed, with postages, tolls, and subscriptions for schools, &c., Notwithstanding all these concessions, the merchants are liable to imprisonment and disgrace at the instance or complaint of a worthless man. When the Badshahi Government is established, all these aforesaid fraudulent practices shall be dispensed with, and the trade of every article, without exception, both by land and water, shall be open to the native merchants of India, who will have the benefit of the Government steam-vessels and steam-carriages for the conveyance of their merchandise gratis; and merchants having no capital of their own shall be assisted from the public treasury. It is therefore the duty of every merchant to take part in the war, and aid the Badshahi Government with his men and money, either secretly or openly, as may be consistent with his position or interest, and forswear his allegiance to the British Government.

Section III—Regarding Public Servants. It is not a secret thing, that under the British Government, natives employed in the civil and military services, have little respect, low pay, and no manner of influence; and all the posts of dignity and emolument in both the departments, are exclusively bestowed on Englishmen for natives in the military service, after having devoted the greater part of their lives, attain to the post of soobadar (the very height of their hopes) with a salary of 60r. or 70r. per mensem; and those in the civil service obtain the post of Sudder Ala, with a salary of 500 r. a month, but no influence, jagheer, or present. . . .

Therefore, all the natives in the British service ought to be alive to their religion and interest, and, abjuring their loyalty to the English, side with the Badshahi Government, and obtain salaries of 200 or 300 rupees per month for the present, and be entitled to high posts in future. If they, for any reason, cannot at present declare openly against the English, they can heartily wish ill to their cause, and remain passive spectators of passing events, without taking any active share therein. But at the same time they should indirectly assist the Badshahi Government, and try their best to drive the English out of the country. . . .

Section IV—Regarding Artisans. It is evident that the Europeans, by the introduction of English articles into India, have thrown the weavers, the cotton dressers, the carpenters, the blacksmiths, and the shoemakers, &c., out of employ, and have engrossed their occupations, so that every description of native artisan has been reduced to beggary. But under the Badshahi Government the native artisans will exclusively be employed in the services of the kings, the rajahs, and the rich; and this will no doubt ensure their prosperity. Therefore these artisans ought to renounce the English services, and assist the *Majahdeens,* engaged in the war, and thus be entitled both to secular and eternal happiness.

Section V—Regarding Pundits, Fakirs and other learned persons. The pundits and fakirs being the guardians of the Hindoo and Mohammedan religions respectively, and the Europeans being the enemies of both the religions, and as at present a war is raging against the English on account of religion, the pundits and fakirs are bound to present themselves to me, and take their share in the holy war. . . .

Lastly, be it known to all, that whoever, out of the above named classes, shall after the circulation of this Ishtahar, still cling to the British Government, all his estates shall be confiscated, and his property plundered, and he himself, with his whole family, shall be imprisoned, and ultimately put to death.

Military Mutiny or National Revolt?

BENJAMIN DISRAELI

One of the earliest analyses of the causes of the war was made by Benjamin Disraeli (1804–1881). As the leading spokesman for the opposition in the House of Commons, he used the news of the troubles in India to attack the policies of the government of Viscount Palmerston, and while his discussion is obviously intended to embarrass his political opponents, it gives a very able statement of a number of important considerations. Disraeli stressed the point that only when the causes of the war were known could suitable measures be taken to restore peace. If, as he contended, the war was not a military mutiny but the symptom of deep discontents among the whole population, then reform of the army system would not meet the dangers threatening British power in India. In his detailed presentation Disraeli demonstrated the careful study he had given to the situation in India, as well as his general bias against the government of the East India Company. For Disraeli, the primary mistake of British rule in India was its increasing tendency to interfere with the established rules and customs. The excerpts given here are taken from a long speech delivered on July 27, 1857, just two months after the first outbreak of violence.

I HAVE always thought if mankind could bring themselves to ponder in time on the commencement of those events that greatly affect their fortunes it is possible that we might bring to the transaction of affairs more prudence and more energy than are generally exercised, and that probably we might prevent many public disasters. It was with that feeling, Sir, when the first news arrived of the occupation of Delhi by the rebels, that I thought I was only performing my duty in addressing some inquiries to Her Majesty's Ministers as to their opinions with regard to the cause of those remarkable events and the exact position of affairs. I am bound to say that at the time the answer which I received impressed me with the feeling that Her Majesty's Ministers did not view the events which had occurred in that spirit which I thought their latent importance demanded. The House will recollect what was the information afforded by the Gov-

ernment on that occasion. . . . The House was favoured with the matured opinion of the Cabinet upon these great events—the Chancellor of the Exchequer informed the House that the revolt of the Bengal army was a sudden impulse, occasioned by superstitious feelings. . . . It was clear from their general tone and from the expressions of persons of authority, . . . that the conduct of the native troops in India was looked upon as a mere military mutiny— that was, I think, the expression that was used on that occasion. Now, I apprehend that it is of the greatest importance to obtain as clear an idea as we can of the causes which have led to these events. . . . It was alleged that, this being a mere military mutiny, all we had to do was to put it down, and when it was put down, then the Government would consider the condition of the Indian army. Now, I humbly think that the question whether it is a mere military mutiny is one of primary im-

Parliamentary Debates, 3rd Series, vol. 147, July 27, 1857, pp. 440–472; speech by Benjamin Disraeli.

portance. Is it a military mutiny, or is it a national revolt? Is the conduct of the troops the consequence of a sudden impulse, or is it the result of an organized conspiracy? The House must feel that, upon the right appreciation of that issue, the greatest of all questions, namely, the measures which the Government ought to adopt, or Parliament ought to sanction, entirely depends. The measures which may be adequate in the case of a military mutiny will not be adequate to cope with a national revolt. The measures which may be perfectly competent to deal with conduct which is only the consequence of sudden impulse will be totally insufficient to deal with conduct which is the consequence of a conspiracy long matured, deeply laid, and extensively ramified. . . . I will, therefore, Sir, to-night presume, with the indulgence of the House, to address them upon two points. I will ask them, first, to inquire what are the causes of the present state of affairs in India; and, when they have arrived at a general conclusion on that point, I will ask them to inquire what are the proper measures, under the circumstances, which should be adopted. . . .

Sir, it is not my intention to-night to trouble the House with any lengthened description of the condition of the Bengal army. I apprehend that, whatever may be the variety of opinions which prevail among us on other subjects, no great difference can exist with regard to this—that the condition of the Bengal army, both as regards discipline and disposition, has been for some time, and was at the time of the revolt, highly unsatisfactory. . . . And there is one reason which, above all others, induces me not to enter into any details upon this branch of the question, because I am persuaded (and I shall offer to-night facts and arguments in support of my opinion) that the conduct of the Bengal army in revolting against our authority was the conduct of men who were not so much the avengers of professional grievances as the exponents of general discontent. I shall show, or endeavour to show, to the House

to-night that our Government in India of late years has alienated or alarmed almost every influential class in the country. I shall show, or endeavour to show, to the House to-night that the mutual suspicions and prejudices between rival religions and different races, which were the cause of segregation between powerful classes in that country, have of late years, in consequence of our policy, gradually disappeared, and that for them has been substituted an identity of sentiments, and those sentiments, I am sorry to say, hostile to our authority. . . .

I now proceed to lay before the House the reasons and facts that have induced me to arrive at the conclusions which I have already stated. Of late years a great change has taken place in the Government of India. In olden days, and for a considerable time—indeed, until, I would say, the last ten years—the principle of our government of India, if I may venture to describe it in a sentence, was to respect Nationality. We often talk now of our conquest of India, and sometimes we are told that it is necessary to re-conquer that country. The conquest of a country inhabited by 150,000,000 of men, in many instances of warlike habits, could at no time have been an easy achievement. Its difficulty must certainly be increased to us after what has occurred, and therefore I think it is of some importance that upon this grave and common idea of conquering India we should have as accurate notions as possible. I deny, Sir, that in a vulgar sense of the words we have ever conquered India. We have taken a part in the military operations which have very frequently been conducted upon a great scale in India. The annals of our warfare in India are glorious. Our arms have been victorious in many signal fields and many brilliant campaigns. We have often triumphed over powerful Sovereigns and baffled skilful and dangerous confederacies. But still our conquest of India in the main has been a conquest of India only in the same sense in which William of Orange conquered

England. We have been called in—this happened very frequently in the earlier periods of our Indian history—by populations suffering under tyranny, and we have entered those kingdoms and principalities to protect their religion and their property. It will be found in that wonderful progress of human events which the formation of our Indian empire presents that our occupation of any country has been preceded by a solemn proclamation and concluded by a sacred treaty, in which we undertook to respect and maintain inviolate the rights and privileges, the laws and customs, the property and religion of the people, whose affairs we were about to administer. Such was the principle upon which our Indian empire was founded; and it is a proud as well as a politic passage in the history of Englishmen, that that principle has been until late years religiously observed. . . . Why did the Mahomedans and the Mahrattas fail in India? The two principal causes of the downfall of those dynasties were—first, that they persecuted the people whom they had conquered on account of their religion; and, secondly, that when their treasuries became empty they confiscated the land of the chief proprietors. England, on the contrary, always came in with a guarantee of their lands, and a solemn engagement not to tamper with their religion. It was by a policy founded upon these principles that our power in India was established. All our great Indian authorities, indeed, have recognized in the existence of independent Native States a source not of embarrassment, but of security to England. They have looked upon them, to use the expression of one of the most eminent of our Indian statesmen, as the "safety valves" of our empire. The turbulent spirits of the country were enrolled in their armies. Their mode of life offered a career which our more regulated and ordinary habits would not have furnished to the fiery youth of India. A strict observance of our treaties, the rigid maintenance of the laws and customs of the people, and, above all, a

faithful respect for our guarantees of their land and a scrupulous adhesion to our engagements not to tamper with their religion —these were the sources of our strength, and upon these our great Indian statesmen always insisted. But, Sir, of late years a new principle appears to have been adopted in the government of India. . . . Everything in India has been changed. Laws and manners, customs and usages, political organizations, the tenure of property, the religion of the people—everything in India has either been changed or attempted to be changed, or there is a suspicion among the population that a desire for change exists on the part of our Government. Now, taking the last ten years, I would range under three heads the various causes which have led, in my opinion, to a general discontent among all classes of that country with our rule. I would describe them thus—first, our forcible destruction of native authority; next, our disturbance of the settlement of property; and thirdly, our tampering with the religion of the people. I believe that directly or indirectly, all the principal causes of popular discontent or popular disturbance will range under those three heads. . . .

Now, Sir, I will first address myself to the forcible destruction of native authority in the East by our Government, and in this subject are involved some of the most important principles of Indian policy. The House must recollect that even at the present time there are at least 200 Native Indian princes; they still govern a population of at least 60,000,000 of inhabitants. With all these princes the English Government has treaties. These treaties differ in many particulars of detail; in some there are conditions for contingents, in others for tribute, in others, again, for the residence at the Native Court of a representative of the English Government; but there is one feature of similarity throughout all these treaties—that is, an engagement on the part of the English Government with each Indian prince, that so long as the latter shall observe the conditions of the treaty, the English Government will secure to him and to his heirs for ever the throne upon which he sits. Now, Sir, about the year 1848 is what I fix as the date of the inauguration of the new system of Indian policy, which I shall show to be opposed to all the principles by which our empire was gained and established. Great wars had then terminated victoriously and triumphantly for this country. The struggles with new Powers that had sprung up— with ancient Powers that had threatened us—were closed. There was no fear of foreign assailants, and under those circumstances less regard for internal safeguards against discontents. But the condition of India, in a financial point of view, was by no means satisfactory. The House is so familiar with this part of the subject that I shall not dwell too closely upon details. The House is aware that the nature of Indian revenue is such that it admits of no expansion. The great bulk of the revenue is raised from the land; and, although we receive a considerable amount from the duties on opium and salt, yet the revenue from those sources in a great degree can only increase from increased consumption by an increased population. Affairs, however, had come to such a point, that it was absolutely necessary that the revenue of the East Indian Government should be enlarged. About this time accordingly appeared one of the most important State papers that ever was published relating to India: it was a Minute of Council referring to the decease of an Indian prince, and in which was laid down the principle, almost without disguise, that the future Indian policy would be, to increase the revenue of our dominions by increasing our dominions themselves; that, in short, the only mode by which an enlarged revenue could be obtained was, by enlarging our territories. . . . The Rajah of Sattara, as I have already reminded the House, died without natural heirs, but the House must also remember that the Hindoo system is such, that a family can never become extinct. . . . The Rajah of Sattara,

dying without natural heirs, had, before his death, selected an heir, who was nominated with all the solemn ceremonies peculiar to the occasion, whose adoption was notified to the British Resident, and published to the people by salvoes of artillery, and was received by them with perfect approbation. The Governor General of India, however, in pursuance of the vigorous and novel policy which he had determined to establish in India, took the decided step of abolishing the law of adoption; he did not recognize the individual who had been proclaimed to all India as the son and successor of the deceased prince: but, claiming the equivocal right of suzerainty, or Lord Paramount, he ordered his troops to enter the Raj, and the Rajah of Sattara was absorbed into the dominions of the East India Company. [*Disraeli then went on to show how the same general principle led to the annexation of the territories of the Raja of Berar.*]

Now, Sir, I must pause here for a moment on the subject of annexation. I want to touch upon the second division of the subject. I want to show you how the settlement of property in India has been disturbed by the new system of Government during the last ten years. This portion of the subject is intimately connected with that part to which I have already adverted, and the House will see in a few moments why I have stopped at the year 1854 on the subject of annexation. Remember, the principle of the law of adoption is not solely the prerogative of princes and principalities in India; it applies to every man in Hindostan who has landed property and who professes the Hindoo religion. . . . What man was safe? What feudatory, what freeholder who had not a child of his own loins was safe throughout India? These were not idle fears; they were extensively acted upon and reduced to practice. . . . Here was a new source of revenue. But while all these things were acting upon the minds of these classes of Hindoos, the Government took another step to disturb the settlement of property. . . . The

House is aware . . . that there are great portions of the land of India which are free from land-tax. Being free from land-tax in India is far more than equivalent to freedom from the land-tax in this country, for, speaking generally and popularly, the land-tax in India is the whole taxation of the State; and it is not a light impost, therefore, by any means. There are large portions of the land in India which enjoy this freedom. The origin of the grants under which these lands are held is difficult to penetrate, but some are undoubtedly of great antiquity. . . . But under the new system established in India this plan of investigating titles was at once embraced, as a proof of a powerful Government, a vigorous Executive, and most fruitful source of public revenue. Therefore, Commissions were issued to inquire into titles to landed estates in the Presidency of Bengal and adjoining territory. They were also issued in the Presidency of Bombay, and surveys were also ordered to be made in the newly-settled or North-Western provinces, in order that these Commissions might be conducted, when the surveys were completed, with due efficiency. Now, there is no doubt that during the last nine years the action of these Commissions of Inquiry into the freehold property of India has been going on at an enormous rate, and immense results have been obtained. . . . I am induced to believe the amount obtained by the Government of India in this manner—that is, by the resumption of estates from their proprietors—is not less in the Presidency of Bengal alone than £500,000 a year. Conceive what a capital is represented by such an annual revenue! Conceive the thousands and tens of thousands of estates that must have been resumed by the Government from the proprietors to obtain such a result! . . . But there is another source of revenue, which during the last few years recourse has been had to, and with respect to which the results, as regards the opinions and sentiments of the population, are not less important. The House will understand that

when we gradually obtained absolute predominance over the great kingdoms of India we often left a nominal authority— the pomp and pageant of power—to the Native Princes, to whom and to their heirs and chief dependents, the Government accorded pensions. They were perpetual pensions. For instance, the Nabob of Arcot, when he ceded the Carnatic, was guaranteed a considerable pension, and this revenue was enjoyed for several generations. I mention this as an illustrative case. Not only the descendants of the chief, but the Ministers and great personages all had pensions, which were placed on the Government list of India. Now, under the new system these pensions have been discontinued, and are to be considered as annuities only. The House will see that this conversion of hereditary pensions into personal annuities is confiscation by a new means, but on a most extensive, startling, and shocking scale, because the descendants of those ancient Royal Families and nobles find themselves by this new rule reduced to a state of the utmost humiliation, and the people see their ancient Sovereigns, whose deposition from political power they might for many reasons feel a loss, reduced almost to absolute beggary. . . . The House will see, therefore, with reference to the second point, how far the Government have disturbed the settlement of property by their conduct with regard to the resumption of lands, by abolishing the principle of adoption, and by changing into annuities those pensions on condition of paying which we became lords of the sovereignties. That, then, I say, is the second great cause which has produced general discontent throughout India, and has estranged numerous and powerful classes from that authority which I think on the whole they were disposed to regard with deference.

Sir, I have now to approach the third point—that of tampering with the religion of the people of India. This, I am aware, is one of those subjects which are called difficult and delicate; but, in my opinion, no subject is difficult or delicate when the existence of an empire is at stake, and I shall therefore address myself to this point without any undue reserve. I know that a great prejudice has been raised in this country against missionary enterprise in India, and if I could ascribe to missionary enterprise in that country any share in the production of those vast calamities which we are now considering, nothing should induce me to shrink from avowing my opinion. When, however, we hear of missionary enterprise in India being the source and origin of these disasters and troubles, I cannot but remember that missionary enterprise is no new feature in India. At a period antecedent to the existence of our empire there were active Christian missions in India. Roman Catholic missions existed, I believe, before the successes achieved by Clive, and although our own missions are of much more modern date, their greatest efforts—their most energetic exertions—have been co-existent with general satisfaction and peace among all classes in India, and with a vigorous and successful policy on the part of the Government. With these facts before me, then, I must hesitate before I attribute to missionary interference any of those calamities and dangers which we are now considering. . . . I think very great error exists as to the assumed prejudices of Hindoos with regard to what is called missionary enterprise. The fact is that the Hindoos, and the Indian population generally, with the exception of the Mussulmans, are educated in a manner which peculiarly disposes them to theological inquiry. . . . So far from the Hindoo looking with suspicion upon the missionaries, I am convinced, from what I have read and heard, that the Hindoo is at all times ready to discuss theological questions with the missionary. . . . But what the Hindoo does dread—what he regards with the utmost jealousy—what he looks upon with undying apprehension— is the union of missionary enterprise with the political power of the Government. . . . No taxation however grievous, no

injustice however glaring, acts so dangerously on the Hindoo character as the persuasion that the authority of the Crown is exercised to induce him to abandon the religion of his forefathers. Now, have the Government of India lent a sanction to that suspicion of the Hindoos? Have the Government taken a course which has led the mass of the people to believe that there was ground for such a suspicion? This is a most important inquiry, and it is one to which the House ought to address itself. I must say, after examining the subject, I am sure with impartiality, that it appears to me that the Legislative Council of India have, under the new system, been constantly nibbling at the religious system of the natives. I do not say that the establishment of a great system of national education—which, if it had been kept free from any taint of this description, would have been of the utmost advantage to India —has been converted into an obvious and open instrument of proselytism. I do not say that in establishing a national system of education for the Hindoos you have gone ostentatiously into their schools with the Sacred Scriptures; but I am very much misinformed if the Sacred Scriptures have not suddenly appeared in those schools; and you cannot persuade the Hindoos that they have appeared there without the concurrence or the secret sanction of the Government. I think also that the establishment of what is called in the Minute "a system of female education in India" was a very unwise step on the part of the authorities. . . . There were, however, other acts on the part of the Government, which I regard as much more reprehensible, and which, as I shall show, have produced very evil consequences. There are two Acts which have passed the Legislative Council of India within the last few years, and which have amazingly disturbed the religious mind of Hindostan. The first was the law which enacted that no man should be deprived of his inheritance on account of a change of religion. That has occasioned great alarm in India. The House must understand that property is inherited in India by men as trustees for sacred purposes, and if a man does not lose his property who has changed his religion some of the principal ends and duties of that inheritance cannot be fulfilled. That is a change in the law which has created much alarm and suspicion. But there is also another law, which has, if possible, more alarmed the feelings of the Hindoos, and that is, the permission to a Hindoo widow to marry a second husband. What could have induced the Governor General of India to pass such a law it is, at this moment, difficult to conceive. If there had been any great feeling on the subject among the Hindoo community, one could have comprehended the reason; but, as I am informed, no man or woman among them ever expressed any desire in favour of a change which is looked upon by all as an outrage on their faith. These two laws have, to my mind, more than any other cause, disquieted the religious feelings of the Hindoos, and prepared their minds for recent lamentable events. . . .

I have now endeavoured to show to the House under the three heads to which I first adverted—namely, the forcible destruction of native authority in India, the disturbance of the settlement of property in India, and the tampering with the religion of India—that there have been causes at work during the last ten years which have naturally and necessarily occasioned great discontent and disquietude among powerful classes in that country. . . . Under these circumstances, I think the House will see that it is no exaggeration to assume that about 1854 and 1855 the temper of India was one of peril, and one which ought to have occasioned disquietude to the Government of that country.

It was under these circumstances . . . that an event occurred in India to the consequences of which I am now going to solicit your attention for a few moments. And that is the annexation of Oude, the effect of which, as I shall show, was of a peculiar and, as regards public opinion, if

I may use the expression, of a generalizing character. . . . We shall be told, no doubt, that the condition of his country was not satisfactory, or that his character was not irreproachable. I shall not enter into these questions. But, whatever may have been thought of his conduct, no right can be founded on that for dethroning him; for by the treaty we had with him the very matter of individual incompetency or misconduct had been anticipated and provided for. . . . However, the moment the throne of Oude was declared vacant, the English troops poured in; the Royal treasury was ransacked, and the furniture and jewels of the King and his wives were seized. From that instant the Mahomedan princes were all alienated. For the first time the Mahomedan princes felt that they had an identity of interest with the Hindoo Rajahs. From that moment they threw aside the sullen pride of former conquerors who would not condescend to sympathize with the victims of Sattara. They saw that from a system founded upon a violation of Hindoo law they were not to be exempted. The moment that the throne of Oude, occupied by its King, was declared vacant, and English troops were poured into his territory, the Mahomedan princes understood what would be their future fate. You see how the plot thickens. You have the whole of the Indian princes—men of different races and different religions—men between whom there were traditionary feuds and long and enduring prejudices, with all the elements to produce segregation—become united—Hindoos, Mahrattas, Mahomedans—secretly feeling a common interest and a common cause. Not only the princes but the proprietors are against you. . . . But the annexation of Oude brought more than all this. Although you had alienated from you the hearts of princes and proprietors—although you had poisoned the former affection and veneration of the peasantry—there was a class in India which, if you had allowed it to remain faithful, might have enabled even the new system to have triumphed. It turned out that the great proportion of the Bengal army were subjects of the King of Oude. I have been told, . . . that there were not less than 70,000 men from Oude in our Indian armies and contingents. They were recruited from the villages; in some instances they were proprietors, in many more they were the sons of proprietors. They entered the service of the British Government. They looked forward, when their period of service terminated, to retire to their native villages with their pensions, and with the high privileges which, if not formally legal, they no less by custom effectually enjoyed. . . . The Oude Sepoy finds that he has no village to return to, where he is to live the favoured subject of his native Sovereign. If he is injured, he must appeal to the Company, and be treated as all other subjects of the Company on the broad plains of Bengal. . . . The Oude Sepoy returns now to his village, and finds it belongs to the Company, and that the rigid revenue system of India is applied to his small property. . . . He finds he has lost political privileges and his territorial position; and, for the first time, the great body of the Bengal army is disaffected. How does that act? With the princes, the proprietors, and the religious classes, all for a long time distrustful and disaffected: the opportunity occurs, and the only class which can keep them in order is angry and discontented. . . . The annexation of Oude took place in 1856. This is only the middle of 1857. Is it true that in the interval there has been no evidence of combination and conspiracy in India? There may have been evidence which the Government has not understood. There may have been symbols which perplexed them. There may have been conduct, the motives of which they could not penetrate. But, that there is no evidence of combination for the last twelve months, especially in Bengal, seems to me a position which cannot for a moment be maintained. The House has heard of the circulation of the mysterious cakes in India—or, if not, allow me to tell them what has taken

place, and was taking place in India many months ago. This took place. A messenger comes to the headman of a village, and brings him six pancakes—*chupatties,* such as the Natives make of wheaten flour—and he says, "These six pancakes are sent to you; distribute them among as many villages, and make six others, and send them on with the same message to another headman." The headman obeys, accepts the six cakes, makes six others, and sends them on to the headman of the next village with the same message. . . . How did it begin? It is a mystery . . . . This sending of cakes went on. I do not say that the Government could penetrate the secret; I do not now find fault with them because they did not find it out.—What I want now to show is—that there were outward and visible signs of confederacy. There was also an indication of conspiracy among the military, which must have been known to the Indian Government. I allude to the circumstance of the lotus flower. A man came with a lotus flower, and gave it to the chief soldier of a regiment. It was circulated from hand to hand in the regiment, and every man who took it looked at it and passed it on, saying nothing. We must understand that every man who passed it on was acquainted with the plot. When it came to the last soldier of the regiment he disappeared and took it to the next station. The process was gone through in every regiment in Bengal. There was not a regiment, not a station, not an escort, among which the lotus flower has not in this way been circulated. All these things took place after the annexation of Oude, and then the Sepoys were drawn into the vortex of that conspiracy which had been long secretly forming. . . . That was certainly significant. I ventured to say that I would show a state of society in India which proved the existence of general discontent, and, difficult as it might be to prove conspiracy, that I would offer to the House facts and circumstances sufficient to convince them that there was conspiracy. I think I have said enough to induce the

House to pause before they form too pre-
cipitate an opinion upon the causes of the
disasters in India. I think I have said
enough to make the House at least feel
that it is not by saying that we have to
deal with a mere military mutiny that we
shall save India. But, I said, and I think
I have shown, that the condition of things
was this—that the people of India were
only waiting for an occasion and a pretext.
That occasion was soon furnished, and
that pretext was soon devised.

Indian Hostility to British Rule

ALEXANDER DUFF

One of the most frequently quoted of the contemporary accounts of the war was written by Alexander Duff (1806–1878), the first missionary sent by the Church of Scotland to India. Duff had been in India since 1830, and, because of the leading part he had taken in the establishment of schools and colleges, he was well-known in Great Britain and America. His reports on the situation in India in the summer of 1857 were made in the form of letters to a friend, and are, as his publishers said, "tense with emotions, and all aflame with the tidings of that terrible season." His special contribution to the historiography of the period is his insistence on the deep-seated hostility of most Indians to British rule. He argued that relations between the two races could only be changed through the spread of Christianity. He was vociferous in his denunciation of the government for its neutral position toward religion.

JULY 2 [1857]. At an early period of this deplorable rebellion I was led, . . . to infer that the cartridge affair and its alleged caste-breaking tendencies were a mere shallow but plausible pretext in the hands of evil-minded, designing men, and that the real originating cause of the whole mischief would be found of a *purely political* character. To this persuasion I gave free expression at a time when few were prepared to entertain it. Every disclosure, however, which of late has been made, goes to demonstrate that it has been the result of a long-concocted Mohammedan conspiracy against the supremacy and rule of Great Britain in India.

Information received from arrested spies and papers found in their possession serves to implicate the ex-King of Oude, and especially his Prime Minister, the Nawab Ali Nukhi Khan, one of the cleverest and wiliest of Asiatic intriguers. Indeed, it is said that since his imprisonment in Fort-William the latter openly avows that he has had a principal share in contriving and working out the deeply-laid plot, and that

he glories in having done so, adding that he has woven a web around the British Government which it will not disentangle for many a day.

To all appearance the titular Emperor of Delhi and members of his family have also been deeply implicated in the dark and foul conspiracy. In time the whole truth may gradually be unfolded. Meanwhile, gleams of light like the following shoot out upon the subject. An officer who escaped from Fyzabad states that, in a conversation with the subadar of his own regiment, the latter said, "As you are going away for ever, I will tell you all about our plans. We halt at Fyzabad five days, and march *via* Darriabad upon Lucknow, where we expect to be joined by the people of the city. Proclamations have been received from the King of Delhi, informing all that he is once more on the throne of his fathers, and calling on the whole army to join his standard. . . ."

[Aug. 26, 1857] While there were doubtless many auxiliary influences at work, every day makes it clearer to all out here

From Alexander Duff, *The Indian Rebellion: Its Causes and Results.* London: James Nisbet, 1858; pp. 46–47, 93, 99–106.

that the tremendous rebellion, in the throes of which we still are, has been the result of a long concocted Mohammedan conspiracy against the British power, with a view to re-establish the old Mogul dynasty instead. It has also been long suspected that Russian spies, under various guises, have been successfully at work in inflaming the bigotry of the Mussulman and the prejudices of the high-caste Hindu. Some disclosures are said to have been made, which may some day throw light on this Russian treachery. Persia, too, under the inspiration of Russia, has also long been suspected of having her agents of mischief among the Mohammedan princes of India. The fact that most of the Mohammedans of Hindustan agree with the Persians in following the *Shia* system of Islamism has tended to strengthen the suspicion. And to-day one of our best-informed journals positively announces that "the Government of Bombay has transmitted to the Supreme Government of India, certain Persian documents addressed to the Khan of Kelat (on the borders of the Punjaub), asking him to give his assistance to the mutineers in expelling the British power." . . .

[Sept. 5, 1857]. As regards the feelings of the great masses of the people towards the British Government, the most contradictory statements have been put forth. Here, as elsewhere, extremes will be found wrong. That there ever was *anything like affection* or *loyal attachment,* in any true sense of these terms, on the part of any considerable portion of the native population towards the British power, is what no one who really knows them could honestly aver. Individual natives have become attached to individual Britons. Of the truth of this statement even the recent sanguinary mutinies have furnished some conspicuous examples. But such isolated facts can prove nothing as to the feelings generally prevalent with respect to the British and their power. On the first subjugation or annexation of a province, the labouring classes, under a fresh sense of the manifold tyrannies, exactions, and disorders from which

they are delivered, usually express satisfaction and delight. But as the first generation dies out, and another rises up, knowing nothing but the even, steady, continuous demands of the British authorities—demands which they cannot evade, as they often might amid the weakness and turbulence of native rule—they are apt to settle down into a state of necessitated acquiescence, or sullen indifference, or latent disaffection and discontent—often secretly sighing for a change of rulers, that might give them some chance of helping or bettering themselves. Such I believe to be the general condition of the people of India, as regards their feelings towards the British and their Government. And such being their condition, any one might anticipate the evolution of conduct which they might be expected to exhibit in the midst of a rebellion, with what must appear to their minds its *doubtful issues.* The quieter and more thoughtful spirits, under dread of ultimate retribution, would hold back, or perhaps show favour or kindness to such Britons as came in their way. The bolder, more resolute, and more impetuous spirits, on the other hand, would at once be ready to sound a jubilee of triumph over the downfall of the British power, and equally ready to display the insolence of triumph over helpless and fugitive Britons. And this I believe to be a tolerably exact picture of the state of feeling and conduct among the native population in the North-West and Central Indian territories towards the British and their rule.

After escaping from the murderous hands of mutineers, British gentlemen and ladies have, in particular instances, experienced kindness at the hands of the common villagers; but in far the greater number of instances they have experienced *quite the reverse.* On this account they have been constantly compelled to shun the villages altogether, and betake themselves to jungles and pathless forests, exposed to the attacks of beasts of prey, and to manifold privations, the narration of which makes one almost shudder. And among the murders ever and anon reported in our public journals, how often do we find this entry opposite a name, *"Killed by the villagers!"* . . . This very day, in one of our public journals, a gentleman, long resident in the interior, thus writes: "I have lost all my property; but my principal object is, to impress upon my countrymen (to convince the Government of this truth seems hopeless) the utter and most virulent hatred the natives have evinced throughout this outbreak, both to our Government and Europeans generally. In every instance where troops have mutinied, they have been joined by the inhabitants, not only of the bazaars, but of the towns and villages adjacent, who not only assisted the sepoys in burning, looting (plundering), and destroying Government property, and that of the European settlers, and all Christians, and in killing any of them they could; but after the departure of the mutineers, continued the devastation, and completed it. . . ."

Now, in the face of these, and scores of other substantially similar statements from all parts of the North-West and Central India, what becomes of the lullaby declarations of those who would fain persuade the British public that nowhere among the general civic or rural population of India does there exist any feeling of ill-will, or discontent, or disaffection, towards the British or their Government? All such unqualified declarations I do most solemnly regard as a gigantic (I do not say wilful) imposition on the British people—an imposition which, if not timeously exposed or abandoned, is sure to prove as fatal to the re-establishment and perpetuity of British supremacy, as it is in itself gigantic. . . .

It is but right, therefore, that the British people should be jealously on their guard against the fair-weather representations of men high in office—men who from personal intercourse know nothing of native sentiment beyond the glozing lies of a few fawning sycophants—men who, from motives of political partisanship and personal self-interest, are sorely tempted to mistake the apparent calm on the upper surface for peace, contentment, and loyalty. It is but right that the British people, to whom the God of Providence has so mysteriously entrusted the sovereignty of this vast Indian empire, should know the real state of native feeling towards us and our power, that they may insist on a searching scrutiny into the causes which may have superinduced it, and, detecting the causes, may demand, as with a voice of thunder, some commensurate remedy. . . . Railways, and telegraphs, and irrigating canals, and other material improvements, *alone* will not do. Mere secular education, sharpening the intellect, and leaving the heart a prey to all the foulest passions and most wayward impulses, will not do. Mere legislation, which, in humanely prohibiting cruel rites and barbarous usages, goes greatly a-head of the darkened intelligence of the people, will not do. New settlements of the revenue, and landed tenures, however equitable in themselves, alone will not do. Ameliorations in the present monstrous system of police and corrupting machinery of law courts, however advantageous, alone will not suffice. A radical organic change in the structure of Government, such as would transfer it exclusively to the Crown, would not, could not, of itself furnish an adequate cure for our deep-seated maladies.

No, no! Perhaps the present earthquake shock which has passed over Indian society, upheaving and tearing to shreds some of the noblest monuments of material civilisation, as well as the most improved expedients of legislative and administrative wisdom, has been permitted, to prove that all merely human plans and systems whatsoever, that exclude the life-awakening, elevating, purifying doctrines of gospel grace and salvation, have impotence and failure stamped on their wrinkled brows. Let, then, the Christian people of the highly-favoured British isles, . . . rise up, . . . let them decree . . . that henceforward those commissioned by them to rule over and administer justice to the millions of this land shall not dare, in their public acts and proclamations, practically to ignore or scornfully repudiate the very name and faith of Jesus, while they foster and honour the degrading superstitions of Brahma and Mohammed. . . . Then, instead of the fiendish howl, with its attendant rapine, and conflagration, and massacre, we shall have millennial songs of gratitude and praise from the hearts and lips of ransomed myriads.

A Military Revolt

SIR JOHN LAWRENCE

In contrast to those observers who, like Alexander Duff, saw the uprisings in the summer of 1857 as evidence of a great conspiracy, or, like Disraeli, saw it as an expression of alarm occasioned among the people by unnecessary reform, there were many who insisted that it was fundamentally an army mutiny. Among those who held this view, few had better sources of information than Sir John Lawrence (1811–1879). He had been appointed assistant-magistrate of Delhi in 1830, then, after holding various other important posts, had become one of three members of the Board that administered the Panjab after its conquest from the Sikhs. In 1857 he was Chief Commissioner and was largely responsible for the coordination and planning that led to the recapture of Delhi. After a few years in England he returned to India as Governor-General (1863–69).

Lawrence was convinced that the real explanation of the war was the inefficiency and lack of discipline in the Bengal Army, and that this could be traced to a considerable degree to the system used for recruiting officers. He also advocated having a larger number of British troops than had been the case before 1857. Reliance on Indian troops for the maintenance of British control was, he believed, a dangerous practice likely to lead to further outbreaks. He expanded on these ideas, while he was actively engaged in the fighting, in a series of letters to Sir Charles Trevelyan, a former member of the Company's Civil Service.

December 16, 1857.
M Y DEAR Trevelyan, Many thanks for your letter of October 20, and kind congratulations. We have just been passing through a frightful ordeal. It is by God's mercy alone that an English person is alive on this side of India. I recognised your old signature (in the "Times") at once. I don't think I saw all your letters, but I did see most of them, and liked all I saw, though I do not think that Delhi would answer for our metropolis, in consequence of its insalubrity. I am glad you do not advocate its destruction. It is a position of great importance, and should be held by us. . . . We have been almost as much to blame for what has occurred as have the people.

I have as yet neither seen nor heard any-thing to make me believe that any conspiracy existed beyond the army; and even in it, one can scarcely say there was a conspiracy. The cartridge question was to my mind, indubitably, the immediate cause of the revolt. But the army had for a long time been in an unsatisfactory state. It had long seen and felt its power. We had gone on, year by year, adding to its numbers, without adding to our European force. Our contingents, which, under better arrangements, might, like the Punjab troops, have acted as a counterpoise, were really a part of the army. All the men were "Poorbeas" [i.e., from Eastern India]. The Bengal army was one great brotherhood, in which all the members felt and acted in union.

Our treasuries, arsenals, forts were all garrisoned by them. As one letter I inter-

From R. Bosworth Smith, *Life of Lord Lawrence*. New York: Scribners, 1883; vol. 2, pp. 251–252, 254.

17

cepted said, it was a *saf mydan* (a clear level) from Delhi to Calcutta, and as a Hindustani observed to a Sikh friend of mine, the proportion of European soldiers to Hindustanis was about equal to the salt a man consumed in his Chupatti. The Mohammedans took advantage of the revolt to convert it into a religious and political affair. The missionaries and indeed religion, really speaking, had nothing to do with the matter. It was an affair of caste, of personal impurity. Both Hindu and Mohammedan believed that we meant by a bit of legerdemain to make them all Christians. Religion, as you know, with them, consists in matters of ceremony. Provided missionaries talked to them without acrimony, I believe they would never have objected to their talking for ever on religion. This, however, only applies to the body of the people, including the soldiers. Of course there are many fanatics. A sense of power, then, defective discipline, and want of sufficient employment ruined the Bengal army. Reform was impracticable, for the officers would not admit that any was necessary, and nobody not in the army was supposed to know anything about it.

I think that we have now weathered the storm. The worst seems over. But great and radical changes are necessary, and who is to effect them? We need a man at the head of affairs of great heart and head, and of vast experience. Nothing short of this will do what is necessary. Condign punishment should of course be meted out to all murderers and the leaders of mutiny. But I see every danger of justice degenerating into revenge of a savage character. Already we hear of strange deeds being perpetrated by private individuals at Delhi and elsewhere. Already it looks too like a general war of white man against black. There is little fear that offenders will escape the just penalty of their crimes; there is much that many innocent people will suffer. It was a great misfortune that troops, even in small numbers, were not sent out overland. Thousands of natives who in the first instance kept aloof, fell off, thinking that our hour was come. They would have sided with us if they had seen a chance; but with the general defection around, and no aid within hail, it was not surprising if they were carried away also.

We should have a European army of at least double its former strength in India, carefully kept up to the maximum strength. The native army should be no greater than is absolutely necessary. It should be officered by men carefully selected and removable simply because they were not successful in the discharge of their duties. The Mutiny Act, as regards native soldiers, should be abolished—at any rate, made to accord with common sense. No man should escape punishment for technical reasons. The officers should be selected in England by competition, as is done with civilians. They should join European corps and learn their duty and habits of discipline, and selections should be made from this body for native corps. Officers so selected should receive extra pay, and so have a strong inducement to exert themselves and give satisfaction. The cry for numbers of officers for native corps is merely a cry for rapid promotion. . . . The police should be reorganised and divided into two bodies—organised police on military principles for guards of gaols, treasuries and the like, and detective police for other duties. The latter will not be benefited by drill. This does not give discipline and moral training, which is what is wanted. Select such men carefully, pay them properly, look after them thoroughly, reward and punish promptly, and you will have good police. So far from being surprised at their faults, I only wonder they did so much as they did. The Sepoys in the army would never have done one-fourth of their work.

April 23, 1858.

My dear Trevelyan, The mail is about to go out, and I have little time to answer your letter of March 11. However, I have often thought over many of the points discussed in your memorandum, and will give you my opinion to the best of my ability.

I am a strong advocate for extending the competition system throughout all branches of the army. I am sure it will work well. As yet, time has not allowed for a fair trial in our Civil Service, but the specimens which it has furnished to the Punjab have been favourable. . . . I think, with Dr. Vaughan, that it is a mistake to think that a clever boy, who has obtained high proficiency at school, cannot be an adept at manly exercises. I think also that mere bookworms are not likely to be candidates for the English services. The circumstance that a boy is willing to come forward and compete for an appointment where the standard is high, is indicative of a certain amount of "grit" in his composition. Moreover, admitting that a few bookworms do find their way into the service, there are parts which will suit them and in which they may do good service. Such men are in every respect superior as public officers to a regular dunce—a thorough hard bargain. . . .

Nothing can be more important than to secure for the army a body of really able officers, of men who have received a good education, and, from boyhood, have been accustomed to use their intellects. With an army so officered it would be impossible for any government to appoint incapable commanders. Public opinion would not permit such abuses. As it is now, mediocrity is the rule of the day; capacity the exception. Public sympathy, even in the army, is in favour of a chief of inferior talents. It is considered cruel to pass him over. Nothing short of a calamity will ensure a proper selection. The zeal, energy, ability, and real experience which prevent misfortune, are seldom to be found in high quarters. . . .

I have always considered that the maximum age for civilians might be reduced with advantage. We want well-educated gentlemen rather than first-rate scholars. Men who come to India at a comparatively mature age, such as clergymen and lawyers, seldom like the country and are apt not to sympathise, as they should do, with the natives. . . .

The Failure of "Divide and Conquer"

KARL MARX

In a later section, two interpretations of 1857 are given by writers influenced by the Marxist understanding of history (see articles by Hutchinson, pages 56–58 and Joshi, pages 59–61). It is interesting to compare these with the views expressed by Karl Marx (1818–1833) in a series of articles he wrote in the summer of 1857 for the New York *Daily Tribune*. In 1853 he had written that British rule in India had destroyed, through free trade, the domestic handicraft industry in India, thus producing "the greatest, and, to speak the truth, the only social revolution ever heard of in Asia." England, he went on to say, in causing this social revolution, "was actuated only by the vilest interests, and was stupid in her manner of enforcing them"; nevertheless "she was the unconscious tool of history in bringing about that revolution." Marx saw the violence of 1857 as an extension of the social process England had already initiated.

THE Roman *divide et impera* was the great rule by which Great Britain, for about one hundred and fifty years, contrived to retain the tenure of her Indian Empire. The antagonism of the various races, tribes, castes, creeds and sovereignties, the aggregate of which forms the geographical unity of what is called India, continued to be the vital principle of British supremacy. In later times, however, the conditions of that supremacy have undergone a change. With the conquest of Scinde and the Punjab, the Anglo-Indian Empire had not only reached its natural limits, but it had trampled out the last vestiges of independent Indian states. . . . It no longer attacked one part of India by the help of another part, but found itself placed at the head, and the whole of India at its feet. . . . The armies at its disposition no longer had to extend its dominion, but only to maintain it. . . . On first view, it is evident that the allegiance of the Indian people rests on the fidelity of the native army, in creating which the British rule simultaneously organized the first general centre of resistance which the Indian people was ever possessed of. How far that native army may be relied upon is clearly shown by its recent mutinies, breaking out as soon as the war with Persia had almost denuded the Presidency of Bengal of its European soldiers. Before this there had been mutinies in the Indian army, but the present revolt is distinguished by characteristic and fatal features. It is the first time that sepoy regiments have murdered their European officers; that Mussulmans and Hindus, renouncing their mutual antipathies, have combined against their common masters; that disturbances beginning with the Hindus, have actually ended in placing on the throne of Delhi a Mohammedan Emperor; that the mutiny has not been confined to a few localities; and lastly, that the revolt in the Anglo-Indian army has coincided with a general disaffection exhibited against English supremacy on the

From Karl Marx, "The Revolt in the Indian Army" and "Dispatches from India," quoted in K. Marx and F. Engels, *The First Indian War of Independence 1857–1859*. Moscow: Foreign Languages Publishing House [n.d.], pp. 40, 56–57.

part of the great Asiatic nations, the revolt of the Bengal army being, beyond doubt, intimately connected with the Persian and Chinese wars.

The alleged cause of the dissatisfaction which began to spread four months ago in the Bengal army was the apprehension on the part of the natives lest the Government should interfere with their religion. The serving out of cartridges, the paper of which was said to have been greased with the fat of bullocks and pigs, and the compulsory biting of which was, therefore, considered by the natives as an infringement of their religious prescriptions, gave the signal for local disturbances. On the 22d of January an incendiary fire broke out in cantonments a short distance from Calcutta. On the 25th of February the 19th Native Regiment mutinied at Berhampore, the men objecting to the cartridges served out to them. . . .

At Benares, an attempt at disarming a native regiment was resisted by a body of Sikhs and the 13th Regular Cavalry. This fact is very important, as it shows the Sikhs, like the Mohammedans, were making common cause with the Brahmins, and that thus a general union against the British rule, of all the different tribes, was rapidly progressing. It had been an article of faith with the English people, that the sepoy army constituted their whole strength in India. Now, all at once, they feel quite satisfied that that very army constitutes their sole danger. During the last Indian debates, Mr. Vernon Smith, the President of the Board of Control, still declared that "the fact cannot be too much insisted upon that there is no connection whatever between the native princes and the revolt." Two days later the same Vernon Smith had to publish a dispatch containing this ominous paragraph:

On the 14th of June the ex-King of Oudh, implicated in the conspiracy by intercepted papers, was lodged in Fort William, and his followers disarmed.

By and by there will ooze out other facts able to convince even John Bull himself that what he considers a military mutiny is in truth a national revolt.

The War as a Russian Plot

DAVID URQUHART

Throughout the nineteenth century many people in Great Britain and India were haunted by the fear of a Russian attack on India; so it is not surprising that Russia's hand was immediately detected in the revolt. Perhaps the most persistent advocate of the idea that Russia was a menace to British interests was David Urquhart (1805–1877), a Member of Parliament who made a reputation as a defender of Turkey at a time when there was considerable criticism in England of Turkish treatment of Christian minorities. For Urquhart, British troubles in India were the product of Russian machinations; and the Russian's chief agents, he insisted, were to be found within the British Cabinet. The quotations are from a pamphlet he wrote criticizing Disraeli's speech on India.

I F THE next mail from India does not announce that the remnant of the English have been driven into the sea, I shall hold it to be, solely because of the superintending providence of Russia, and the extent and efficiency of the agency she has in time established throughout Hindustan.

I suppose it will not be questioned that I have stated in anticipation, and under circumstances which seemed to defy all possibility of prior judgment, the events which have taken Europe by surprise. The method which I have adopted on those occasions, and which will be found very simple, is, to find first, what, in a given case, would be advantageous for Russia; secondly, what could be done towards this advantage by the Minister of France or England? The result gives what will happen. That result is certain if the figures are exact, for Russia is systematic, and the Cabinets of Europe are her tools. Let us here make the application.

It was desirable for Russia that the power of England should be *shaken;* it was not desirable for Russia that it should be *overthrown.* The English Government could act in such a manner as to shake the British dominion in India; having so shaken it, it could no longer control events. What has happened? An insurrection provoked by an act of the English Government. What will

happen? The revolutionary combination will be disconcerted. By concerting it Russia has the means of paralysing it, so it was in Europe in 1848.

An Indian Officer writes 16th July: "Your prophecy regarding India, has turned out more of a reality than most of us expected, for never were we so taken by surprise. There will be tough work before confidence is established. The season of the year will go further towards disabling the Europeans, than the harm the natives can do us—but such a systematic mutiny was never dreamt of, and *it is not a native head that has organised it.*" . . .

Were the English dominion simply to cease, independent dominions would arise: the states intervening between India and her frontier would relapse into the position they occupied prior to 1838, and so far as she was concerned, a common federation would be instituted, which would blast at once the labours and desires of centuries, and snatch from her grasp the prey at the moment it was about to close upon it. By the prolongation of the contest she mutually exhausts the native populations of India and Great Britain; she arouses the hatred on their part, which ultimately must bring her on the field as their protector; she places herself in the same relation towards England, and so finally subdues England at Calcutta, and Europe in Asia.

From D. Urquhart, *The Rebellion of India.* London: D. Bryce, 1857, pp. 21–22.

The Lessons to Be Learned

ANONYMOUS

To many observers the most obvious cause of the widespread antagonism manifested toward the British in 1857 was the work of Christian missionaries. In their attempts to convert the people of India, they had, it was alleged, aroused bitter hostility by their attacks on both Hinduism and Islam. Because of the strong emotions aroused by the charge, perhaps none of the other factors that contributed to the revolt is as difficult to assess in terms of actual importance as this one. On the one hand, it is evident that Hindus and Muslims might very well have been deeply offended at the interpretations given of their religious faith by many Christians. Furthermore, that Indians would be unable to discriminate between the activities of the British in the private capacity of agents of missionary societies and of the British as administrators, would be almost certain, given the social traditions of people unfamiliar with the western dichotomy between church and state. Unfortunately, however, we have little real evidence one way or the other of just what the reaction of people was to the missionary enterprise, since the most vocal opponents of missionaries both in England and India were not any more trustworthy witnesses than were the missionaries themselves. Later statements on the role of missionaries will be found in Part III.

The following selection, taken from an article published where the fighting was still going on, attempted to defend the missionaries against the charges made against them, and, by the way of rebuttal, argued that the war indicated the need for rethinking British attitudes to India.

An alleged cause of disaffection has been education and missionary labours. We believe it is universally admitted —at least, we have not heard any one deny it—that the class of natives educated in Government Colleges, and there carefully protected from all Christian teaching, are to a great extent infidel in creed and dangerous in politics. But, on the other hand, we cannot, at this moment, recollect any pamphlet, or any book, in which it is asserted that the pupils of missionary schools have generally displayed those characteristics. On the contrary, we are inclined to believe that were the English power to come to its final struggle to-morrow, among its best and last native friends would be no small number of these. It must be remembered, that in every case the education received at the hands of the Missionaries has been sought by the natives themselves. Their schools have always been more frequented than those of the Government, or any others; and this simple fact is the one practical answer to all the theory, which asserts that missionary operations, in the way of education or otherwise, must create disaffection.

That the Brahmins foresee that the effect of missionary labours will be the overthrow of their own system is undoubted; for in such a matter they have a truer instinct than the class of English politicians who are their apologists, and who, while they on the one hand charge the Missionaries with turning India upside down, are continually affirming on the other that they will never acquire influence. The Brahmins, on the contrary, know that they will; that the sermon, the book, the school, are surely and irresistibly working their way into the heart of the nation; and doubtless many of them would be glad, on this as on every other account, to see the end of British domina-

"The Sepoy Rebellion," in *The London Quarterly*, XVII, October, 1857.

tion. But all the enemies of Missions—and they are many, bitter, and certainly free from scruples—although they have ventured on the largest assertions, in the highest places, have yet failed to produce one authentic *fact* to prove that the labours of the Missionaries, either in schools or otherwise, have involved the Government in conflict with the people. . . .

Take two extremes of the Indian community—the classes who have been most brought into contact with Missionaries, and those who have been the least. The latter are the Sepoys, and, above all, the Sepoys of the Bengal army. No Missionary ever dared to preach in their lines, or open a school among their children; no Christian native dared to enlist with them. They were studiously kept, by statesmen, from all means of knowing what Christianity really was; and the consequence is, that they are so ignorant of its spirit and aims, as to be the dupes of men who represent our Government as capable of entering into a conspiracy, to break their caste by making them eat hog's lard. . . .

On the other hand, just as enmity to the English has broken out in the classes least approached by Missionaries, and in the countries least occupied by them, so, where their labours are most extensive, and their converts most numerous, British life is at this moment most sacred, and British authority strongest. There have been no risings against the English in Tinnivelly or Travancore in the south, none in Serampore or Krishnagur in the north. In all the Madras Presidency, which has had much more of missionary labour, and had it longer, than any other part of the country, there has been no disaffection; and we will venture to assert, that in proportion as the natives have been under missionary influence, so will they be friendly and serviceable to the English. . . .

Is there any proof in the conduct of the Sepoys of a special desire for the blood of the Missionaries? Even in the sacred city of Benares they have escaped, while many an officer who, poor fellow, was far enough

from offence on the score of Christianity, has been laid low. . . . Only at three stations have we yet heard of Missionaries being killed, and that, we will venture to say, not from special enmity to them, but because nothing European was to be spared. No solitary Mission station has been, so far as we know, attacked. Again, the native newspapers, in their endeavours to prove a conspiracy against the caste of the people, did not allege anything that the Missionaries did, but the action of the authorities— their mad action of thrusting unclean grease on the lips of Brahmins and Mohammedans.

If we turn for a moment to look at the effects of this mutiny, one of the first and most obvious will be, a better knowledge in Europe of Hindu character. It was the fashion of a certain school to paint that character as so gentle, that the atrocities of this rebellion took the public by surprise. But no one familiar with the best writers upon India—with such writers as Orme or Mill—ever expected that Hindus in warfare would act otherwise than they have acted. Feebleness and ferociousness easily unite in the same person. Any one who had read the accounts of Bengal dacoity, or gang robbery, would know that even the most cringing of all the Hindu nations habitually indulge in incredible atrocities, when once engaged in conflict. The authentic memoirs of any native Court, whether Hindu or Mussulman, would be too horrible for belief in England. It is impossible to calculate the saving of human life which has resulted from the British conquest, if it was only through the stopping of murders by authority. We know a case of one Rajah, now deposed, of whom his former subjects say that he killed only five thousand persons while he was on the throne; whereas his father had killed about ten thousand; and his uncle, a much greater and abler man than either, who in his day rendered services to the Government of the Marquis of Wellesley, had killed at least fifteen thousand. . . .

Another effect will be, a clearer apprehension on the subject of native institutions, especially that of caste. This has been hitherto regarded rather as an oriental curiosity than as a bad institution, a practical curse to mankind. By the horrors of this rebellion, many will be taught that caste is the most unnatural barrier ever interposed between man and man, the greatest source of estrangement between neighbours of the same race and language, and the most dangerous obstacle to intercourse between different nations. It must henceforth be looked at gravely as one of the worst things existing under the sun; not to be rudely assailed, because that would rouse fanaticism in its defence, but to be calmly and strongly passed by, in every arrangement let alone, all ordinances and regulations proceeding upon the basis given us by our own constitution, and leaving, in the enjoyment of their rights, those who prefer the pride of caste to the advantages we offer them: and these will be very few; for when the Hindus are not forced, they easily slide into practices irreconcilable with caste, if any advantage is to be gained thereby. . . .

Another effect of the rebellion is, to scatter for ever the confident belief which nearly all the English residents in India entertained, that the Hindus and the Mussulmans could never combine. On this point no one can reproach his neighbour; for all were agreed, and all have been equally disappointed. . . . Henceforth our policy can never take, as the basis of any one proceeding, the assumption that the Hindu and the Mussulman cannot make common cause against us. That hitherto all-pervading element in the calculation of Indian policy must wholly disappear.

Another effect, closely allied with this one, is the proof, terribly perfect now, that the policy of our Government in matters of religion has been a total failure. That policy has been, in its public principles, purely atheistical. As a Government, to have no religion at all, and to support Hinduism for the Hindus, Mohammedanism for the Mohammedans, and Christianity for the English, with a view to please all, has been the way of our Government. Our whole Indian policy has been tinged with the original character of commerce. We have traded in everything, from crowns down to cowry-shells, and from opium up to conscience. Which would cost least, or which would pay most, has always been the ruling consideration. Meaner than any conquerors in any country before, we have been ashamed and afraid to avow and encourage our own creed. Our authorities did all that in them lay to keep Hindus and Mussulmans in complete ignorance of Christianity. They did more: they did all that in them lay to excite the jealousy of the natives against Christian efforts to enlighten them. They sowed fear and discontent, by manifesting disfavour to their own religion to obtain the confidence of the Hindus. Even with an honest and straightforward people, such conduct could not obtain respect; but to those who can never believe in the integrity of any one, so deeply is their own character imbued with dissimulation, all these evidences of tremor or anxiety could have but one meaning; they were adopted to hide a conspiracy. Had the Government been as honest as the Mussulmans when they were in power, or . . . as any kind of rulers that the Hindus have ever had to do with before—that is, had they avowed, and acted on, and encouraged their own religion—the whole body of Hindus would by this time have known what that religion and its principles are, and been persuaded that to it the idea of obtaining crowds of nominal adherents, by fraud or force, would be utterly abhorrent. . . .

Again, one of the most immediate results will be, the revival in the native mind of the old dread of British valour. For years we have ceased to meet native hosts with small bands; our armies, from the days of Lord Hastings down, have assumed proportions which complimented every enemy with the show of meeting him on equal terms; and besides, European and Sepoy qualities have been confounded, the fire of the British regiment inspiring its neighbour, the soul of the British officer animating his men. In this state of things, the deeds done by handfuls of English in the heroic days of Clive and Lawrence, Wellesley and Lake, had faded from the native memory; and many Sepoy regiments probably thought themselves quite a match for British ones. Their first trial at Meerut seemed to justify such an idea. But since that day, how often has the brow of the rebel darkened and furrowed with terror, as he heard the tale of what tens and twenties of Britons have done! Five hundred attacking ten thousand, and frightening them away, as at Agra; a handful holding Lucknow against all the forces of the kingdom; another handful holding Cawnpore; less than three hundred scattering three thousand at Benares; and the fearful charges of the Rifles at Delhi, when, ten against a hundred, they dash forward with the cry, "Remember the Ladies—Remember the Babies," and everything flies before them: these are feats which heroes can appreciate, and which cowards will feel to the depths of their soul. . . .

Against such tales they can set those of women ripped, mutilated, stripped naked, sold by auction, burned alive; babies hacked and cast into the flames; husbands mutilated, and compelled to witness the dishonour of their wives; but none of heroism or prowess. They have never gained an action in the open field, no matter what their odds; never carried a position against British arms, no matter how few. Their success has been only by murder, not once by victory. In the history of the world there never was a rebellion with such means and advantages, which effected so little. . . .

But some ulterior plans will soon present themselves before us, and demand our judgment, and require our prompt approval and our firm support. When the trouble is past, what then? What is to be the future policy of England in India? Is it to be a temporizing, hollow, half-Hindu policy, attempting to bolster up an insecure power, by cloking our national faith and princi-

ples? or is it to be a manly English policy, taking our stand as what we are, rulers; rulers now by double right, and well-tested strength; rulers who have a character which we proclaim to be higher than that of the people we rule, a religion more enlightened, laws and institutions more benign, and a will which we mean shall command? . . .

We look steadily into the future. The trial long past, the new order established, and what then? Our comfort is that the destiny of India will be hastened by this awful providence. When a great work is to be accomplished for which mere human measures are hopelessly inadequate, the Almighty is wont to interpose by extraordinary means—by means which man could not conceive and dare not execute; from which we first shrink in terror before we bow to them in gratitude. Perhaps it is so in the case of this terrible visitation. Mercy not only "seasons justice," but inspires it. Nothing less than a sword to "go through the land" will plough up the field for the reception of humanizing and immortal truths. Nothing but a social earthquake could break up that system of consolidated wrongs which we call India. The curse of its native rule was the twofold curse of idolatry and oppression; it has groaned for ages under the tyranny of "gods many and lords many." And now that we are about more thoroughly to supersede the rapacious and cruel rule of its chiefs, it will behove us to put to shame its foolish and obscene "divinities" by the exhibition of a purer worship. If we take the country and its people for our beloved Queen, shall we not put both it and them under the protection of the same true God? It is only as we are faithful henceforth to the spirit of our own institutions, civil and religious, that we may profit by this dreadful lesson, and hope to see the slow but steady light of prosperity advance above the plains and heights of Hindustan.

PART II: THE JUDGMENTS OF THE VICTORS

The War as a Brahmanical Protest

SIR JOHN KAYE

Sir John Kaye (1814–1876), one of the most prolific writers on the history of the British connection with India, was convinced that the main cause of the rebellion in 1857 was fear on the part of the Brahmans of the innovations introduced by the British. Unlike other observers who had come to somewhat the same conclusion he did not regard this fear as either unjustified or as a reflection on the character of British rule. As the traditional guardians of Hindu culture, the Brahmans, according to Kaye, understood the threat posed to their religion and to their own privileged position by the advance of Western civilization. They had taken the lead, therefore, in instigating the soldiers and the general populace to revolt. In this understanding, the war was seen as the last desperate efforts of the Brahmans to defend themselves against the forces of modernity.

T HE whole hierarchy of India saw their power, their privileges, and their perquisites rapidly crumbling away from them, and they girded themselves up to arrest the devastation.

All this had been going on for years; but the progress of enlightenment had been too slow, and its manifestations too little obtrusive, greatly to alarm the sacerdotal mind. As long as the receptacles of this new wisdom were merely a few clever boys in the great towns, and the manhood of the nation was still saturated and sodden with the old superstition, Brahminism might yet flourish. But when these boys grew up in time to be heads of families, rejoicing in what they called their freedom from prejudice, laughing to scorn their ancestral faith as a bundle of old wives' fables, eating meat and drinking wine, and assuming some at least of the distinguishing articles of Christian apparel, it was clear that a very serious peril was beginning to threaten the ascendancy of the Priesthood. They saw that a reformation of this kind once commenced, would work its way in time through all the strata of society. They saw that, as new provinces were one after another brought under British rule, the new light must diffuse itself more and more, until there would scarcely be a place for Hindooism to lurk unmolested. And some at least, confounding cause and effect, began to argue that all this annexation and absorption was brought about for the express purpose of overthrowing the ancient faiths of the country, and establishing a new religion in their place.

Every monstrous lie exploded, every abominable practice suppressed, was a blow struck at the Priesthood; for all these monstrosities and abominations had their root in Hindooism, and could not be eradicated without sore disturbance and confusion of

From Sir John Kaye, *A History of the Sepoy War in India 1857–1858*. London: W. H. Allen, 1864, pp. 183–191.

the soil. The murder of women on the funeral-pile, the murder of little children in the Zenana, the murder of the sick and the aged on the banks of the river, the murder of human victims, reared and fattened for the sacrifice, were all religious institutions, from which the Priesthood derived either profit, power, or both. Nay, even the whole-sale strangling of unsuspecting travellers was sanctified and ceremonialised by religion. Now all these cruel rites had been suppressed, and, what was still worse in the eyes of the Brahmins, the foul super-stitions which nurtured them were fast dis-appearing from the land. Authority might declare their wickedness, and still they might exist as part and parcel of the faith of the people. But when Reason demon-strated their absurdity, and struck convic-tion into the very heart of the nation, there was an end of both the folly and the crime. The Law might do much, but Education would assuredly do much more to sweep away all these time-honoured superstitions. Education, pure and simple in its secularity, was quite enough in itself to hew down this dense jungle of Hindooism; but when it was seen that the functions of the Eng-lish schoolmaster and of the Christian priest were often united in the same person, and that high officers of the State were present at examinations conducted by chaplains or missionaries, a fear arose lest even secular education might be the mask of proselytism, and so the Brahmins began to alarm the minds of the elder members of the Hindoo community, who abstained, under priestly influence, from openly countenancing what they had not the energy boldly to resist.

And, every year the danger increased. Every year were there manifestations of a continually increasing desire to emancipate the natives of India from the gross supersti-tions which enchained them. One common feeling moved alike the English Govern-ment and the English community. In other matters of State-policy there might be es-sential changes, but in this there was no change. One Governor might replace an-other, but only to evince an increased hostil-ity to the great Baal of Hindooism. And in no man was there less regard for time-hon-oured abominations and venerable absurd-ities—in no man did the zeal of iconoclasm work more mightily than in Lord Dal-housie. During no former administration had the vested interests of Brahminism in moral and material error been more ruth-lessly assailed. There was nothing system-atic in all this. Almost, indeed, might it be said that it was unconscious. It was simply the manifestation of such love as any clear-sighted, strong-headed man may be sup-posed to have for truth above error, for intelligent progress above ignorant stagna-tion. From love of this kind, from the assured conviction that it was equally hu-mane and politic to substitute the strength and justice of British administration for what he regarded as the effete tyrannies of the East, had emanated the annexations which had distinguished his rule. And as he desired for the good of the people to extend the territorial rule of Great Britain, so he was eager also to extend her moral rule, and to make those people subject to the powers of light rather than of darkness. And so he strove mightily to extend among them the blessings of European civilisation, and the Priesthood stood aghast at the sight of the new things, moral and material, by which they were threatened.

Many and portentous were these men-aces. Not only was Government Education, in a more systematised and pretentious shape than before, rapidly extending its net-work over the whole male population of the country, but even the fastnesses of the female apartments were not secure against the intrusion of the new learning and new philosophy of the West. England had be-gun to take account of its short-comings, and, among all the reproaches heaped upon the Company, none had been so loud or so general as the cry that, whilst they spent millions on War, they grudged hundreds for purposes of Education. So, in obedience to this cry, instructions had been sent out to India, directing larger, more comprehen-sive, more systematic measures for the instruction of the people, and authorising increased expenditure upon them. Whilst great Universities were to be established, under the immediate charge of the Government, the more humble missionary institutions were to be aided by grants of public money, and no effort was to be spared that could conduce to the spread of European knowledge. It was plain to the comprehension of the guardians of Eastern learning, that what had been done to unlock the floodgates of the West, would soon appear to be as nothing in comparison with the great tide of European civilisation which was about to be poured out upon them. . . .

About the same time the wedge of another startling innovation was being driven into the very heart of Hindoo Society. Among the many cruel wrongs to which the womanhood of the nation was subjected was the institution which forbade a bereaved wife ever to re-marry. . . . Evil and cruel would it have been in any country and under any institutions, but where mere children are married, often to men advanced in years, and are left widows, in tender youth, when they have scarcely looked upon their husbands, its cruelty is past counting. To the more enlightened Hindoos, trained in our English colleges and schools, the evils of this prohibition were so patent and so distressing, that they were fain to see it abrogated by law. . . . It was plain that the innovation would inflict another deadly blow on the old Hindoo law of inheritance. Already had dire offence been given to the orthodoxy of the land by the removal of those disabilities which forbade all who had forsaken their ancestral faith to inherit ancestral property. A law had been passed, declaring the abolition of "so much of the old law or usage as inflicted on any person forfeiture of rights or property, by reason of his or her renouncing, or having been excluded from, the communion of any religion." Against this the old Hindoos had vehemently protested, not without threats, as a violation of the pledges given by the British Government to the natives of India; pledges, they said,

issued in an hour of weakness and revoked in an hour of strength. But Lord Dalhousie had emphatically recorded his opinion "that it is the duty of the State to keep in its own hands the right of regulating succession to property," and the Act had been passed. And now there was further authoritative interference on the part of the State, for it was proposed to bestow equal rights of inheritance on the offspring of what the old-school Hindoos declared to be an illicit, God-proscribed connexion. . . .

Nor was it only by the innovations of moral progress that the hierarchy of India were alarmed and offended. The inroads and encroachments of physical science were equally distasteful and disquieting. A privileged race of men, who had been held in veneration as the depositaries of all human knowledge, were suddenly shown to be as feeble and impotent as babes and sucklings. It was no mere verbal demonstration; the arrogant self-assertion of the white man, which the Hindoo Priesthood could contradict or explain away. There were no means of contradicting or explaining away the railway cars, which travelled, without horses or bullocks, at the rate of thirty miles an hour, or the electric wires, which in a few minutes carried a message across the breadth of a whole province.

These were facts that there was no gainsaying. He who ran might read. The prodigious triumphs over time and space achieved by these "fire-carriages" and "lightning-posts," put to shame the wisdom of the Brahmins, and seemed to indicate a command over the supernatural agencies of the Unseen World, such as the Pundits of the East could never attain or simulate. They, who for their own ends had imparted a sacred character to new inventions, and had taught their disciples that all improvements in art and science were derived from the Deity through their especial intercession, and were to be inaugurated with religious ceremonies attended with the usual distribution of largesses to the priests, now found that the white men could make the very elements their slaves, and call to their aid miraculous powers undreamt of in the Brahminical philosophy. Of what use was it any longer to endeavour to persuade the people that the new knowledge of the West was only a bundle of shams and impostures, when any man might see the train come in at a given moment, and learn at Benares how many pounds of flour were sold for the rupee that morning in the bazaars of Delhi and Calcutta?

Was There a Conspiracy?

G. B. MALLESON

One of the most debated aspects of the war of 1857 is the nature of the Indian leadership. In contrast to the opinion generally held by almost all modern historians that there was no really coordinated advance planning is the view that a widespread and well-organized conspiracy had been at work for some years plotting the overthrow of the British. The most persuasive exponent of this interpretation was George Bruce Malleson (1825–1898), author of many historical works on India. Malleson had gone to India as a cadet in the military service of the East India Company in 1842, but later became the correspondent for the London *Times*.

    Malleson identified three principal figures as leaders of the conspiracy: Nana Sahib, the adopted son of the last Peshwa, the leader of the Marathas; Maulavi Ahmad-allah, a Muslim religious leader; and the Rani of Jhansi, the widow of a ruler of a small state in Central India. While Malleson's arguments are carefully worked out, they frequently are based on a confusion of cause and effect, and on the assumption that his three figures actually controlled events. His studies of 1857 are of great importance, however, for an understanding of the later nationalist historians, since writers like Savarkar (see Section III) used his materials for their own reconstruction.

THERE was a large amount of seething discontent in many portions of India. In Oudh, recently annexed; in the territories under the rule of the Lieutenant-Governor of the North-west Provinces, revolutionised by the introduction of the land-tenure system of Mr. Thomason; in the Southern Máráthá territory, the chiefs of which had been exasperated to the very verge of revolt by an inquiry, instituted under the auspices of a commission, called the Inám Commission, into the titles of estates which they and their forefathers had held without question since the beginning of the century, men's minds were excited and anxious. Suddenly, shortly after the annexation of Oudh, this seething discontent found expression. . . . Conspirators to work upon so promising a soil were not wanting to the occasion. . . . Who all the active conspirators were may probably never be known. One of them, there can be no question, was he who, during the progress of the Mutiny, was known as the Maulavi [A Muslim religious leader]. The Maulavi was a very remarkable man. His name was Ahmad-ullah, and his native place was Faizábád in Oudh. In person he was tall, lean, and muscular, with large deep-set eyes, beetle brows, a high aquiline nose, and lantern jaws. Sir Thomas Seaton, who enjoyed, during the suppression of the revolt, the best means of judging him, described him "as a man of great abilities, of undaunted courage, of stern determination, and by far the best soldier among the rebels." Such was the man selected by the discontented in Oudh to sow throughout India the seeds which, on a given signal, should spring to active growth. Of the ascertained facts respecting his action this at least has been proved, that very soon

From George Bruce Malleson, *The Indian Mutiny of 1857*. New York: Scribners, 1891, pp. 17–19, 27–33.

after the annexation of Oudh he travelled over the North-west Provinces on a mission which was a mystery to the European authorities; that he stayed some time at Agra; that he visited Dehlí, Mírath, Patná, and Calcutta; that, in April 1857, shortly after his return, he circulated seditious papers throughout Oudh; that the police did not arrest him; that the executive at Lakhnao, alarmed at his progress, despatched a body of troops to seize him; that, taken prisoner, he was tried and condemned to death; that, before the sentence could be executed, the Mutiny broke out; that, escaping, he became the confidential friend of the Begum of Lakhnao, the trusted leader of the rebels.

That this man was the brain and the hand of the conspiracy there can, I think, be little doubt. During his travels he devised the scheme known as the chapátí scheme. Chapátís are cakes of unleavened bread, the circulation of which from hand to hand is easy, and causes no suspicion. The great hope of the Maulaví was to work upon the minds, already prone to discontent, of the sipáhís. When the means of influencing the armed men in the service of the British Government should have been so matured that, on a given signal, they would be prepared to rise simultaneously, the circulation of chapátís amongst the rural population of the North-west Provinces would notify to them that a great rising would take place on the first favourable opportunity.

It is probable that, whilst he was at Calcutta, the Maulaví, constantly in communication with the sipáhís stationed in the vicinity of that city, discovered the instrument which should act with certain effect on their already excited natures. It happened that, shortly before, the Government of India had authorised the introduction in the ranks of the native army of a new cartridge, the exterior of which was smeared with fat. These cartridges were prepared in the Government factory at Dam-Dam, one of the suburbs of Calcutta. The practice with the old paper cartridges,

used with the old musket, the "Brown Bess," already referred to, had been to bite off the paper at one end previous to ramming it down the barrel. When the conspirators suddenly lighted upon the new cartridge, not only smeared, but smeared with the fat of the hog or the cow, the one hateful to the Muhammadans, the other the sacred animal of the Hindus, they recognised that they had found a weapon potent enough to rouse to action the armed men of the races which professed those religions. What could be easier than to persuade the sipáhís that the greasing of the new cartridges was a well-thought-out scheme to deprive the Hindu of his caste, to degrade the Muhammadan? . . . They had been told that the object of their foreign masters was to make them all Christians. The first step in the course to Christianity was to deprive them of their caste. This end could be accomplished insidiously by the defilement to be produced by biting the greased cartridge. Existence without a religion was in their minds intolerable. Deprived of their own, having become outcasts by their own act, they must, in despair, accept the religion of their masters. . . . No sooner had it become certain that this idea had taken a firm root in their minds than chapátís passed from village to village in the rural districts of the North-west Provinces, announcing to the population that grave events were impending for which it became them to be prepared. . . .

I have already referred to the action of the Maulaví of Faizábád as being instrumental in creating and increasing the undercurrent of hostility to British rule through Bengal and the North-west Provinces. It is impossible, however, to leave this subject without mentioning the action of the son of the ex-Peshwá, Bájí Ráo [Nàná Sáhib]. . . . It is the more necessary that such mention should be made, because, whatever may be the opinion of Europeans saturated with the western ideas, and with the conceit those ideas often engender, there can be no doubt but that, during the Mutiny, on the morrow of the

Mutiny, and at the present day, the cultivated natives of India attributed and attribute a great deal of the bitterness attendant on the uprising to the treatment meted out to Nàná Sáhib by the Government of India. I know that it has been contended, and recently most ably contended, that that treatment was absolutely just. It was just according to western ideas. But the oriental mind does not admit of the validity of an agreement which deprives a man of his kingdom and makes no provision for his family after his death. Such was the grievance of Nàná Sáhib. He had no title in law. But the natives of India believed then, they believe still, that he had a moral claim superior to all law. . . .

Nàná Sáhib appealed to the Court of Directors against the decision of the Governor-General of India. . . . Their reply emulated in its curtness and its rudeness the answer given by Lord Dalhousie. They directed the Governor-General to inform the memorialist "that the pension of his adoptive father was not hereditary, that he has no claim whatever to it, and that his application is wholly inadmissible." The date of the reply was May 1853. It bore its fruit at Kánhpur in June 1857. . . .

Not very far distant from Agra there was a powerful chieftain who, from causes similar to those which had influenced Nàná Sáhib, regarded herself as having been grievously wronged, and who therefore hated the English with all the bitterness of a woman who had been contemned. This chieftain was the Ráni of Jhánsí. She was largely gifted, possessed great energy, had borne, up to the period upon which I am entering, "a high character," being "much respected by everyone at Jhánsí." But the hand of the despoiler had lashed her into a fury which was not to be governed. Under Hindu law she possessed the right to adopt an heir to her husband when he died childless in 1854. Lord Dalhousie refused to her the exercise of that right, and declared that Jhánsí had lapsed to the paramount power. In vain did the Ráni dwell upon the services which in olden days the rulers of Jhánsí had rendered to the British Government, and quote the warm acknowledgments made by that Government. Lord Dalhousie was not to be moved. He had faith in his legions. With a stroke of his pen he deprived this high-spirited woman of the rights which she believed and which all the natives of India believed, to be hereditary. That stroke of the pen converted the lady, of so high a character and so much respected, into a veritable tigress so far as the English were concerned. For them, thereafter, she would have no mercy. There is reason to believe that she, too, had entered into negotiations with the Maulaví and Nàná Sáhib before the explosion of 1857 took place.

The executive council of this conspiracy had arranged, in the beginning of 1857, to act upon the sipáhís by means of the greased cartridge, upon the inhabitants of the rural districts by the dissemination of chapátís. This dissemination was intended as a warning that the rising was imminent. It was further decided that the rising of the sipáhís should be simultaneous, and more than once the actual day was fixed. Providentially something always happened to prevent the explosion on that day. The splutterings which occurred on such occasions served to give timely warning to the Government. The delays which followed the warning were partially utilised. It was not, however, till the rising actually took place at Mírath that the Government realised the real nature, though not the full extent, of the danger. That they never realised it thoroughly until after the massacre of Kánhpur we have the evidence of their own words and their own actions to prove. Indeed I may go so far as to declare that many of the actors in the drama failed to realise to their dying day that the outbreak was not merely a mutiny which they had to combat, but a vast conspiracy, the threads of which were widely spread, and which owed its origin to the conviction that a Government which had, as the conspirators believed, betrayed its trust was no longer entitled to respect or allegiance.

The Massacre of Cawnpore

GEORGE O. TREVELYAN

Accounts of fearful atrocities committed by the rebelling soldiers spread rapidly in 1857. The newspapers both in India and Great Britain were filled with gruesome narratives of the butchering of children and the raping of English women in the streets of Delhi. While many of these stories were demonstrably false, they form an important element in the understanding of British attitudes, for this emphasis on Indian atrocities was one of the dark legacies of the struggle. Another point of view is seen in the writings of Section III.

Most famous of all the stories was that of the Well of Cawnpore, where the bodies were thrown of the women and children who had been prisoners of Nana Sahib, one of the leaders of the rebellion. For many British, Cawnpore became a symbol of the depravity of the people whom they ruled, and was of special importance since, unlike many similar accounts, the details were essentially true.

Sir George Otto Trevelyan (1838–1928) son of a Governor of Madras and nephew of Lord Macaulay, traveled through Northern India five years after the restoration of British control. His account of Cawnpore is written in a quiet style that heightens the horror of his story. At the point where the selection given here begins, he has told how the English women and children of the surrounding districts had been imprisoned by Nana Sahib in a small building at Cawnpore.

ABOUT half-an-hour after this the woman called "the Begum" informed the captives that the Peishwa [Nana Sahib] had determined to have them killed. One of the ladies went up to the native officer who commanded the guard, and told him that she learned they were all to die. To this he replied that, if such were the case, he must have heard something about it; so that she had no cause to be afraid: and a soldier said to the Begum: "Your orders will not be obeyed. Who are you that you should give orders?" Upon this the woman fired up, and hurried off to lay the affair before the Nana. During her absence the sepoys discussed the matter, and resolved that they would never lift their weapons against the prisoners. One of them afterwards confessed to a friend that his own motive for so deciding was anxiety to stand well with the Sahibs, if ever they got back to Cawnpore. The Begum presently returned with five men, each carrying a sabre. Two were Hindoo peasants: the one thirty-five years of age, fair and tall, with long mustachios, but flat-faced and wall-eyed: the other considerably his senior, short, and of a sallow complexion. Two were butchers by calling: portly, strapping fellows, both well on in life. The larger of the two was disfigured by the traces of the smallpox. They were Mahommedans, of course; as no Hindoo could adopt a trade which obliged him to spill the blood of a cow.

These four were dressed in dirty-white clothes. The fifth, likewise a Mussulman, wore the red uniform of the Maharaja's body-guard, and is reported to have been the sweetheart of the Begum. He was called

From George Otto Trevelyan, *Cawnpore*. London: Macmillan, 1865, pp. 332–336. Reprinted by permission.

Survur Khan, and passed for a native of some distant province. A bystander remarked that he had hair on his hands.

The sepoys were bidden to fall on. Half-a-dozen among them advanced, and discharged their muskets through the windows at the ceiling of the apartments. Thereupon the five men entered. It was the short gloaming of Hindostan—the hour when ladies take their evening drive. She who had accosted the officer was standing in the doorway. With her were the native doctor, and two Hindoo menials. That much of the business might be seen from the verandah, but all else was concealed amidst the interior gloom. Shrieks and scuffling acquainted those without that the journeymen were earning their hire. Survur Khan soon emerged with his sword broken off at the hilt. He procured another from the Nana's house, and a few minutes after appeared again on the same errand. The third blade was of better temper: or perhaps the thick of the work was already over. By the time darkness had closed in, the men came forth and locked up the house for the night. Then the screams ceased: but the groans lasted till morning.

The sun rose as usual. When he had been up nearly three hours the five repaired to the scene of their labours over-night. They were attended by a few sweepers, who proceeded to transfer the contents of the house to a dry well situated behind some trees which grew hard by. "The bodies," says one who was present throughout, "were dragged out, most of them by the hair of the head. Those who had clothes worth taking were stripped. Some of the women were alive. I cannot say how many: but three could speak. They prayed for the sake of God that an end might be put to their sufferings. I remarked one very stout woman, an half-caste, who was severely wounded in both arms, who entreated to be killed. She and two or three others were placed against the bank of the cut by which bullocks go down in drawing water. The dead were first thrown in. Yes: there was a great crowd looking on: they were standing along the walls of the compound. They were principally city people and villagers. Yes: there were also sepoys. Three boys were alive. They were fair children. The eldest, I think, must have been six or seven, and the youngest five years. They were running round the well (where else could they go to?) and there was none to save them. No: none said a word, or tried to save them."

At length the smallest of them made an infantile attempt to get away. The little thing had been frightened past bearing by the murder of one of the surviving ladies. He thus attracted the observation of a native, who flung him and his companions down the well. One deponent is of opinion that the man first took the trouble to kill the children. Others think not. The corpses of the gentlemen must have been committed to the same receptacle: for a townsman who looked over the brink fancied that there was "a Sahib uppermost." This is the history of what took place at Cawnpore, between four in the afternoon of one day and nine in the morning of another, almost under the shadow of the church-tower, and within call of the Theatre, the Assembly Rooms, and the Masonic Lodge. Long before noon on the sixteenth July there remained no living European within the circuit of the station.

Toward a Consensus

T. RICE HOLMES

That the British public continued to evince a considerable interest in the events of 1857 is evidenced by the many editions and reprintings of the standard work, *A History of the Indian Mutiny* by Thomas Rice Holmes (1855–1933). First published in 1883, it is essentially a detailed narrative history, but Holmes also tried to show the causes that had precipitated the violence. His summary, which is quoted here, represents the interpretation that had become fairly generally accepted by the end of the century. He finds no indication of conspiracy or of a national uprising, but he sees the events as the product of groups who feared the beneficent changes being introduced by the new administration.

THE objects of this chapter are to determine, from the evidence recorded in the preceding narrative, first, what were the causes of the Mutiny and of the disturbances which accompanied it among the civil population, and secondly, what was the significance of those disturbances, whether, in short, they amounted to rebellion. . . . For historical purposes the evidence is amply sufficient.

The evidence concerns first, the mental attitude of the natives of India, and particularly of the subjects of the Company, before the outbreak of the Mutiny, and secondly, their conduct during its progress.

History and common sense alike show that a rebellion, properly so-called, can never take place without provocation. Had the British Government given such provocation? It is true that, on personal grounds, the King of Delhi, minor potentates who were alarmed by the progress of annexation, landholders who had suffered from the unwise action of the British Government, ambitious spirits whom its levelling policy had condemned to restless inaction, all who fancied that its overthrow would open to them opportunities for gratifying their selfish desires, desired that overthrow with more or less eagerness. So did many Mahomedans from political or religious motives, and many Brahmins from a sense of wounded self-importance. There were others too, who, though they did not perhaps consciously desire the ruin of the Feringhees, were yet so far dissatisfied with them and their administration, that they would not have been sorry to see them involved in difficulties. But, though British rule had been far from faultless, it was confessedly superior to any that had preceded it: the poor and the unwarlike knew that it had ameliorated their lot; and its sins had not been grave enough to provoke deliberate rebellion. The accident that it was an alien and infidel rule, however humiliating to native pride, would never have been enough in itself to afford provocation. The result of this absence of provocation, coupled with the diversities of race, religion, rank, status, and aim among the discontented, was that they neither wished nor were able to combine against the British Government. They were

From T. Rice Holmes, *A History of the Indian Mutiny*. London: Macmillan, 1913, pp. 556–560. Reprinted by permission.

simply in a mood to take advantage of any embarrassment which might overtake it, for the attainment of their private ends: some of them were in a mood to scheme, and did scheme, in order to bring such embarrassment upon it.

Excepting the General Service Enlistment Act and the new postal rules, the native army had, in the beginning of 1857, hardly any substantial grievances to complain of: but the relaxation of discipline had encouraged them to twist into a grievance anything that startled their imaginations, or offended their caprices. They were irritated by past acts of bad faith: they sympathised with civil discontent; and they shared in the general fear, begotten of ignorance, that Religion was in danger. They were from various causes generally far less attached to their British officers than they had once been: it was in the nature of things impossible that, without such attachment, they should feel active loyalty towards the British Government; and they had become so powerful and were so conscious of their power that, from purely selfish causes, they were ripe for mutiny.

While the feelings of the civil and military populations of India were in this inflammable condition, the discovery of the greased cartridge struck them like a flaming brand hurled into a mass of stored gunpowder; the inevitable mutiny burst forth; the zealots or sufferers who really desired to sweep the British away, took up arms against them, or waited in the hope that it would soon be safe to strike; the discontented seized the opportunity to redress their grievances; and many who were not discontented were swept away by sympathy, by threats, by persuasions, or by greed, into the flood of disaffection, or like schoolboys who, though prepared to reverence authority, must find a vent for their inborn love of mischief when they feel that their master is powerless to control them, took advantage of the prostration of governmental force to outrage the law. But, as might have been expected, the dis-

turbances, except in one or two isolated regions, and on the part of a few embittered or fanatical groups, never amounted to rebellion. If they had done so, the empire must have been destroyed.

In trying to estimate the conduct of the people of India during the Mutiny, it is important to bear in mind that it would have been unnatural for them to feel towards an alien Government like ours the loyalty that can only co-exist with patriotism. Those of them who regarded our rule as beneficial helped us, or at least left us free to help ourselves; but there was hardly one of them who would not have turned against us, if he had once come to believe that we should be overthrown. Such conduct might not have accorded with romantic notions of fidelity; but it would most certainly have been dictated by common sense. No wise man ever fights for a lost cause. If we had not been able to quell the Indian Mutiny, it would have been a plain proof that we had no business to be in India.

Although, even in Dalhousie's time, the sepoys were in a mutinous temper, although their fears and hopes were probably excited by the agents of discontented princes, it is certain that, before the greased cartridge story got abroad, they formed no definite plot for a general mutiny. Whether or not such a plot was formed afterwards, will never be ascertained: all that is certain is that, in the spring of 1857, a correspondence was kept up among the regiments of the Bengal army, and that they generally agreed to refuse the cartridges.

The evidence clearly proves that Dalhousie was not in any special degree, not more than any one else, responsible for the Mutiny, or for the disturbances which accompanied it. It is true that some of the acts of his administration, righteous though they were, had added to the discontent which produced some of the disturbances. But that the harsh criticisms directed against the annexation policy by pamphleteers and historians were unsound is demonstrated by the fact that, with two exceptions, the annexed states were far less disturbed in the years of the Mutiny than provinces which had been for generations under British rule. The exceptions were Oudh and Jhánsi. It is certain that, if those states had not been annexed, the British Government would have escaped some of the difficulties which beset it in 1857 and 1858; but it would have purchased this relief by infamy—the infamy of abandoning millions of peasants to groan under oppression for fear of incurring the ill-will of their oppressors. Moreover, even the annexations of Oudh and Jhánsi would have been harmless, if they had been supported, as they would have been by any Government but ours, with armed force. Nor must it be forgotten that the rebellion in Oudh was due, not so much to annexation, as to the want of judgement with which the tálukdárs were treated after the annexation; and still more to the failure of Havelock's first two attempts to relieve Lucknow; to the abandonment of Lucknow by Sir Colin Campbell; to the blunders which he committed during the siege; and to Canning's proclamation. On the other hand, Dalhousie had pleaded earnestly for an increase of the European force, which, if it had been granted, would have greatly strengthened his successor's hands, and might have averted the direst calamities of the Mutiny; while by the construction of roads, railways, and telegraphs, and above all by the magnificent administration which he had bestowed upon the Punjab, he had contributed so much to the power by which order was restored to India that he deserved to be mentioned with gratitude rather than with reprobation.

The question still remains, how far the rulers of India were to blame for the evils which befell them and so many of their subjects. The Mutiny might doubtless have been prevented, if the native army had been treated with invariable consideration and good faith, if discipline had been persistently enforced, and if the due proportion between the numbers of the European and native troops had been maintained. But, if a general mutiny had ever been suffered to break forth, no power on earth could have prevented quasi-rebellious disturbances from following it. Just as the lawless and tyrannical barons of the twelfth century took advantage of the feebleness of Stephen to plunder and oppress their weaker neighbours, and chafed against the strong and just rule of Henry Plantagenet; just as a general mutiny of the London police would be followed by a violent outburst of crime on the part of the London thieves and roughs; so would the tálukdárs [landlords], the dispossessed landholders, the Gujars, and the budmashes [criminals] of India have welcomed the first symptom of governmental weakness as a signal for gratifying their selfish instincts. The worst that can be alleged against our rule is that we had, with the best intentions, made many mistakes, which intensified the force of the disturbances occasioned by the Mutiny: but much of the discontent felt against us was the inevitable result of measures which, rightly taken on behalf of the suffering many, had offended the tyrannical few, much of it had been aroused by that resolute assertion of the majesty of the law which is the first duty of every Government.

PART III: REREADING THE EVIDENCE

The Indian War of Independence

V. D. SAVARKAR

The analyses of the nature and causes of the war that had been made by British writers were challenged in 1909 by a young Indian writer in a work that has played a remarkably influential role in the development of modern Indian historiography. Vinayak Damodar Savarkar (1883–) grew up in Western India at a time when a new attitude was making itself felt in India. The founders of the Indian National Congress, the first organization to make a concerted effort to gain Indians a larger share in the government of their country, had depended upon the British to respond willingly to their appeal for a gradual reform. By 1900, however, there were many voices, particularly in Western India and in Bengal, who were saying that freedom would never be won by oratory; that it would be necessary for India to appeal to violence.

Savarkar was one of a group of students who went to Europe to learn such revolutionary techniques as the making of bombs and the planning of political assassinations. But he realized that something more than the destruction of the British was needed: Indians must be filled with the desire to rise against their oppressors. It was for this reason that he wrote his account of 1857, calling it "the Indian War of Independence." While it would be impossible to openly advocate the violent overthrow of the Government, an account of a previous struggle for freedom would, he believed, be quite as effective in inspiring the people to armed revolt.

Savarkar's book, which was printed in Holland, was immediately proscribed by the British authorities, but nevertheless copies of it were smuggled into India, and even those who never read it began to think of the revolt of 1857 as a great national war of liberation. This interpretation was widely accepted by the nationalist movement, and all later writers on the history of India in the nineteenth century have been forced to examine Savarkar's arguments.

MAZZINI, in a critical article on Carlyle's *French Revolution,* has said that every revolution must have had a fundamental principle. Revolution is a complete re-arrangement in the life of historic man. A revolutionary movement cannot be based on a flimsy and momentary grievance. It is always due to some all-moving principle for which hundreds and thousands of men fight, before which thrones totter, crowns are destroyed and created, existing ideals are shattered and new ideals break forth, and for the sake of which vast masses of people think lightly of shedding sacred human blood. The moving spirits of revolutions are deemed holy or unholy in proportion as the principle underlying them is beneficial or wicked. As in private life, so also in history, the deeds of an individual or a nation are judged by the character of the motive. If we forget this test, we cannot appreciate the vast difference between the empire-building wars of Alexander the Great and Italy's fight for liberty under Garibaldi. Just as to decide about the merits of these two dif-

From "An Indian Nationalist," *The Indian War of Independence of 1857.* London: 1909, pp. 4–9, 62–63, 68–69, 71, 77, 81. Reprinted by permission.

ferent events one has to consider the prime motive of the chief actors in those wars, so also to write a full history of a revolution means necessarily the tracing of all the events of that revolution back to their source—the motive, the innermost desire of those who brought it about. This is the telescope which will show clearly the lights and shadows obscured by the blurred presentation of partial and prejudiced historians. When a beginning is made in this manner, order appears in the apparent chaos of inconsistent facts, crooked lines become straight, and straight lines appear crooked, light appears where darkness is, and darkness spreads over light, what appeared ugly becomes fair and what looked beautiful is seen to be deformed. And expectedly, or unexpectedly, but in a clear form, the Revolution comes into the light of real history.

The history of the tremendous Revolution that was enacted in India in the year 1857 has never been written in this scientific spirit by any author, Indian or foreign. And hence there are current throughout the world most extraordinary, misleading, and unjust ideas about that Revolutionary War. English authors have committed, in this respect, all the faults noted above. Some of them have not made any attempt beyond merely describing the events, but most of them have written the history in a wicked and partial spirit. Their prejudiced eye could not or would not see the root principle of that Revolution. Is it possible, can any sane man maintain, that that all-embracing Revolution could have taken place without a principle to move it? Could that vast tidal wave from Peshawar to Calcutta have risen in flood without a fixed intention of drowning something by means of its force? Could it be possible that the sieges of Delhi, the massacres of Cawnpore, the banner of the Empire, heroes dying for it, could it ever be possible that such noble and inspiring deeds have happened without a noble and inspiring end? Even a small village market does not take place without an end, a motive; how, then,

can we believe that that great market opened and closed without any purpose—the great market whose shops were on every battlefield from Peshawar to Calcutta, where kingdoms and empires were being exchanged, and where the only current coin was blood? No, no. The market was neither opened nor closed without a purpose. English historians have always ignored this point, not because it is difficult to ascertain it, but because it is against their interests to admit the truth.

Even more deceptive than this indifference, and one which changes or distorts the whole spirit of the Revolution of 1857 is the other device of English historians copied by their Indian sycophants—the device, namely, of describing the rumour as to the greased cartridges as the moving cause of the Revolution. An Indian writer drawing inspiration from English history and English money says, "Foolish people went mad simply at the rumour that cartridges were greased with cows' and pigs' fat. Did anyone inquire as to whether the report was true? One man said and another believed; because the second became disaffected, a third joined him, and so like a procession of blind men, a company of inconsiderate fools arose, and rebellion broke out." We propose to discuss later on whether people blindly believed the rumour about cartridges. But it will be plain to anyone who has read even the English historians closely and thought about the matter, that a great attempt has been made to father all the responsibility of the Revolution on this rumour. It is not surprising that to one, who thinks that a mighty rising like that of '57 can be produced by such trifles, it was only "a company of inconsiderate fools." If the Revolution had been due only to the cartridges, why did Nana Sahib, the Emperor of Delhi, the Queen of Jhansi, and Khan Bahadur Khan of Rohilkhand join it? These were not surely going to serve in the English army, nor were they compelled to break the cartridges with their teeth! If the rising were due wholly or chiefly to the cartridges, it would have stopped suddenly as soon as the English Governor-General issued a proclamation that they should not be used any more! He gave them permission to make cartridges with their own hand. But instead of doing so, or ending the whole by leaving the Company's service altogether, the sepoys rose to fight in battle. Not only the sepoys but thousands of peaceful citizens and Rajas and Maharajahs also rose, who had no direct or indirect connection with the army. It is therefore clear that it was not these accidental things that roused the spirit of sepoy and civilian, king and pauper, Hindu and Mahomedan.

Equally misleading is the theory that the rising was due to the annexation of Oudh. How many were fighting, taking their lives in their hands, that had no interest whatsoever in the fortunes of the Oudh dynasty? Then, what was their motive in fighting? The Nabob of Oudh himself was imprisoned in the fort of Calcutta; and according to the English historians, his subjects were very much disaffected under his regime. Then, why did Talukdars, soldiers, and almost every one of his subjects unsheath their swords for him? A "Hindu" of Bengal wrote an essay in England at that time about the Revolution. In it the "Hindu" says, "You have no idea how many simple and kindhearted people who had never seen the Nabob, nor were ever again likely to see, wept in their huts when the sorrows of the Nabob were being related before them. And you do not also know how many soldiers were daily taking an oath, after the tears had flown, to avenge this insult on Wajid Ali Shah, as if a calamity had fallen on themselves in person." Why did the Sepoys feel this sympathy with the Nabob and why did eyes which had never seen the Nabob glisten with tears? It is plain, therefore, that the Revolution did not break out simply on account of the annexation of Oudh.

The fear of greased cartridges and the annexation of Oudh were only temporary and accidental causes. To turn these into real causes would never help us in understanding the real spirit of the Revolution. If we were to take them as the real moving causes, it would mean that, without these, the Revolution would not have taken place —that without the rumour of greased cartridges and without the annexation of Oudh, the Revolution would not have been there. It would be impossible to find a theory more foolish and more deceptive. If there had been no fear of the cartridges, the principle underlying that fear would have cropped up in some other form and produced a Revolution just the same. Even if Oudh had not been annexed, the principle of annexation would have manifested itself in the destruction of some other kingdom. The real causes of the French Revolution were not simply the high prices of grain, the Bastille, the King's leaving Paris, or the feasts. These might explain some incidents of the Revolution but not the Revolution as a whole. The kidnapping of Sita was only the incidental cause of the fight between Rama and Ravana. The real causes were deeper and more inward.

What, then, were the real causes and motives of this Revolution? What were they that they could make thousands of heroes unsheath their swords and flash them on the battlefield? What were they that they had the power to brighten up pale and rusty crowns and raise from the dust abased flags? What were they that for them men by the thousand willingly poured their blood year after year? What were they that Moulvies preached them, learned Brahmins blessed them, that for their success prayers went up to Heaven from the mosques of Dehli and the temples of Benares?

These great principles were Swadharma [one's duty] and Swaraj [self-government]. In the thundering roar of "Din, Din," which rose to protect religion, when there were evident signs of a cunning, dangerous, and destructive attack on religion dearer than life, and in the terrific blows dealt at the chain of slavery with the holy desire of acquiring Swaraj, when it was evident that chains of political slavery had been put round them and their God-given liberty wrested away by subtle tricks—in these two, lies the root-principle of the Revolutionary War. In what other history is the principle of love of one's religion and love of one's country manifested more nobly than in ours? . . . They might be darkened for a time by the mist of slavery—even the sun has its clouds—but very soon the strong light of these self-same principles pierces through the mist and chases it away. Never before were there such a number of causes for the universal spreading of these traditional and beautiful principles as there were in 1857. These particular reasons revived most wonderfully the slightly unconscious feelings of Hindusthan, and the people began to prepare for the fight for Swadharma and Swaraj. In his Proclamation of the establishment of Swaraj, the Emperor of Delhi says, "Oh, you sons of Hindusthan, if we make up our mind we can destroy the enemy in no time! We will destroy the enemy and will release from dread our religion and our country, dearer to us than life itself!" What is holier in this world than such a Revolutionary War, a war for the noble principles propounded in this sentence, "release from dread our religion and our country, dearer to us than life itself"? The seed of the Revolution of 1857 is in this holy and inspiring idea, clear and explicit, propounded from the throne of Delhi, THE PROTECTION OF RELIGION AND COUNTRY. In the Proclamation issued at Bareilly, he says "Hindus and Mahomedans of India! Arise! Brethren, arise! Of all the gifts of God, the most gracious is that of Swaraj. Will the oppressive Demon who has robbed us of it by deceit be able to keep it away from us for ever? Can such an act against the will of God stand for ever? No, no. The English have committed so many atrocities that the cup of their sins is already full. To add to it, they have got now the wicked desire to destroy our holy religion! Are you going to remain idle even now? God does not wish that you should remain so; for he has in-

spired in the hearts of Hindus and Mahomedans the desire to turn the English out of our country. And by the grace of God, and your valour, they will soon be so completely defeated that in this our Hindusthan there will not remain even the least trace of them! In this our army, the differences of small and great shall be forgotten, and equality shall be the rule; for, all who draw the sword in this holy war for the defence of religion are equally glorious. They are brethren, there is no rank among them. Therefore, I again say to all my Hindi brethren, 'Arise and jump into the battlefield for this divinely ordained and supreme duty!' " The man who, after seeing such magnificent utterances by the Revolutionary leaders, does not understand its principles is, as we said, either a fool or a knave. What stronger evidence is needed to prove that Indian warriors drew their swords at the time for Swadharma and Swaraj, feeling it the duty of every man to fight for the rights given to man by God? These Proclamations issued at different times and places during the War make it unnecessary to dilate more on its principles. These Proclamations were not issued by nonentities; but they were orders issued from adorable and powerful thrones. They were burning expressions of the agitated feelings of the time. In these the real heart of the nation had spoken out, when at the time of war, there was no occasion to conceal real sentiments through pressure or fear. This tremendous, heroic shout, "Swadharma and Swaraj," proclaims to the world the character of the Revolution in which "all who draw the sword are equally glorious." . . .

[*Savarkar then argued that this zeal for self-government found leadership in Nana Sahib, the adopted son of the last Maratha Peshwa.*]

[Nana] studied the conditions of his country, saw the sufferings of his countrymen, noticed the destruction of his religion and, diagnosing all these chronic symptoms, he came to the conclusion that nothing but the sword could cure that terrible disease of slavery. Though it is not clear what was the ultimate ideal which he set before himself, still, it would appear that, in his opinion, the first thing to do was to drive the English out by unsheathing the sword and thus get independence; and then, to nurture and protect Swadesh under the banner of the united authority of all the Indian princes. . . . Nana's programme was first to fight a united fight, to make India free and, by removing internecine warfare, to establish the rule of the United States of India which would, thus, take its rightful place in the council of the free nations of the earth.

He, also, felt that the meaning of "Hindusthan" was thereafter to be the Swadesh of the adherents of Islam as well as Hinduism. As long as the Mahomedans lived in India in the capacity of rulers, so long, to be willing to live with them like brothers was to acknowledge national weakness. Hence, it was, up to then, necessary for the Hindus to consider the Mahomedans as foreigners. But this rulership of the Mahomedans, Guru Govind in the Panjab, Rana Pratap in Rajputana, Chhatrasal in Bundelkhand, and the Mahrattas, by even sitting upon the throne at Delhi, had destroyed; and, after a struggle of centuries, Hindu sovereignty had defeated the rulership of the Mahomedans and had come to its own all over India. It was no national shame to join hands with Mahomedans now, but it would, on the contrary, be an act of generosity. So, now, the original distinction between the Hindus and the Mahomedans was laid to eternal rest. Their present relation was one not of rulers and ruled, foreigner and native, but simply that of brothers with the one difference between them of religion alone. For, they were both children of the soil of Hindusthan. Their names were different, but they were all children of the same Mother; India therefore being the common mother of these two, they were brothers by blood. . . .

How to achieve this ideal was the one all-absorbing thought of everyone in the palace of Brahmavarta. Two things were necessary for the success of this terrible war that was to be waged to win back freedom. The first thing was to create a passionate desire in Hindusthan for this ideal; the second was to make all the country rise simultaneously for the purpose of achieving it. To turn India's mind into the channels of freedom and to guide India's hand to strike for freedom, these two things it was necessary to accomplish; and this in such a manner that the Company's government should not suspect anything while the scheme was yet unripe. . . . A secret organisation was resolved upon at once . . .

To obtain all information about this secret society, either now or in the immediate future, is as difficult as it is to obtain the information about any other secret society. But upon the facts that occasionally come to light, one cannot but admire the skill of the organisers.

A little before 1856, Nana began to send missionaries all over India to initiate people into this political ideal. In addition to sending missionaries to awaken the people, Nana also sent tried and able men to the different princes from Delhi to Mysore, to fill their minds with the glorious ideal of the United States of India and to induce them to join in the Revolution. These letters, which were sent into every Durbar secretly, clearly pointed out how the English were playing the game of reducing India to insignificance by annexing Swadeshi kingdoms under the pretext of "no heir," how those states which were spared yet would soon be reduced to the same fate as the others and how, under the yoke of slavery, country and religion were both being trampled under foot; and they concluded by exhorting the princes to work for the Revolution which was to make them free. . . .

It was the custom to have a Mullah and a Pundit in every regiment for religious purposes. Taking advantage of this, the Revolutionaries entered the service as regimental Mullahs and, at the falling of the night, used to preach Revolution to the Sepoys secretly. Thus, these political Sanyasis toured from village to village for two years preaching Revolution, and at last succeeded in sowing the seeds of the terrible war to come.

While itinerant Sanyasis and itinerant preachers preached in the villages and the country, local preachers were being sent to the bigger towns. In all the important places of pilgrimage where thousands of people congregated, the ever-existing dumb dislike of the usurping Feringhi rule was intensified into active hatred by the Revolutionary preachers. . . .

In order to make clear to the common people, in simple and clear language, how Swadharma and Swatantra—Religion and Independence—were being insulted, the all-comprehensive programme of the Revolutionary party had not left out of their consideration any of the festivals . . . in which people took interest and congregated in large numbers. The dolls in the doll-theatres began now to speak a strange language and to dance a dangerous dance. . . .

Everywhere was this hatred of slavery and the desire for Swaraj manifested. "My religion is dying, my country is dying: my people have been reduced to a condition worse than that of dogs!"—such were the fears that moved every heart; and an unconquerable desire arose in every heart, from prince to pauper, to make that country live and that people rise to the height of men. And the passionate conviction went forth that streams of blood were but a small price to achieve that independence. . . .

To instil into every heart the one great desire for independence, and rouse it to action, there could be no more effective weapon than poetry. . . . The principal court bard of the Emperor of Delhi had himself composed a national song which was to be sung by every throat in Hindusthan, and the Emperor of Delhi, in person, had ordered that this should be sung on all occasions of public ceremony.

It described the heroic deeds of the past and painted a pathetic picture of the present fallen state. . . .

While the national song was educating the people about their past glory and their present fall, a prophecy, that emblazoned the star of future hope and encouraged all, was heard, in the land. Prophecies are the leaps of the mind into the future. As soon as the heart of India began to long for Swaraj, the prophecies too began to point to Swaraj. From the northern snows to the extreme south, young and old circulated the prophecy that, thousands of years ago, a holy, ancient sage had foretold that the Feringhi *Raj* would end exactly a hundred years from the date of its creation! Indian newspapers gave wide publicity to this prophecy and interpreted it to mean that the Company's *Raj* would fall to pieces on the 23rd of June, 1857. This one prophecy led to the performance of such wonders in Hindusthan that it may safely be asserted that, but for this prophecy, several portions of this history would have to be written in a different way altogether. The year 1857 was the centenary of the Battle of Plassey and the Company's rule would end in that year—this idea created a strange hope and an extraordinary inspiration which moved every part of Hindusthan since the beginning of 1857. . . .

Not alone in the revolutions of Russia, but in the Revolution in India, too, the police were found to be in sympathy with the people. The programme, then, of the civil officers was to join secretly in the Revolutionary organisation of their countrymen without giving up government service and, when the right time came, to work on under Swarajya, performing those very functions which they were all doing under the English government.

Now that the wheels of the secret machinery of the Revolution were set in motion, it was necessary to arrange that all the various motions should be synchronised. With this purpose, in Bengal, a messenger of the Revolutionaries went to the cantonments, taking a red lotus in his hand. He would give the red lotus into the hands of the chief Indian officer in the first regiment. The chief would pass it on to the nearest Sepoy. The Sepoy would pass it to the one next to him, and so the red lotus would pass from Sepoy to Sepoy through the hands of all the thousand Sepoys, and then the last Sepoy would return it back to the Revolutionary messenger. That was enough! Without a whisper or a word, the messenger would pass on like an arrow and, as soon as the next regiment was in sight, he would give the red lotus in the hands of its chief officer. In this way, the organisation, so full of poetry, became impressed with one opinion, with revolution, with blood. The red lotus was the final seal of the organisation. What a tumult of thoughts must be raging in the mind of every Sepoy when he touched the red flower! That courage which it would have been impossible for the eloquence of orators to inspire was imparted in those warlike fellows by the dumb lotus flower and by the mute eloquence of its red, red colour. . . .

Ready! Friends, be ready! And, O unfortunate Tyranny sleeping unconsciously and proud on the green, green hills, be ready too! O world! Our India has certainly patience as its prominent feature; but do not, on that account, take undue advantage, for within the body of this India, whose treasure is all-forbearing calmness, resides concealed, the terrible power of burning, too. . . . Hast thou ever beheld a volcano! Apparently it is clothed with soft green vegetation; but let it once open its jaws, and then all sides will begin to pour forth boiling lava. But now this living volcano of Hindusthan . . . has begun to boil. Terrible streams of lava in its interior are bubbling up tumultuously. Dangerous mixtures of explosive chemicals are being formed, and the spark of the love of liberty has fallen on it. Let Tyranny take a warning when it is not yet too late! Neglect it in the least, and a thunderous explosion would tell insolent Tyranny what volcanic vengeance really means!

The Political Theory of the Indian Mutiny

F. W. BUCKLER

An interesting interpretation of the events of 1857 was given by F. W. Buckler, an English historian, at a meeting of the Royal Historical Society in 1922. According to Buckler, the war has been misunderstood because it was seen as either a revolt or a nationalist uprising when in fact it was neither. The clue to the meaning of the war was to be found, he argued, in the legal relationships that existed between the East India Company and the Mughal Emperors. According to Buckler, the Company had accepted the role of vassal, but in 1843 the Governor-General, by refusing to offer the customary present, severed the original bond that bound the East India Company to the Emperor. What followed was not a revolt by the Company's soldiers, but a return of soldiers to their King against the rebellious Company.

Buckler's argument is logically worked out, but he does not put forward any evidence to show that the Bengal Army was aware of the distinctions he makes. It is a valuable argument, however, as a corrective to the common assumption that Indian monarchy was unsupported by political theory.

T HE "Mutiny" was the summary of the rise of the British in India, and, as the cry of the Sepoys at Meerut was "Delhi, Delhi," it is in Delhi that the key to a political theory must be sought. The scope of this paper is limited, therefore, to the light thrown upon the subject by "the proceedings of the trial of the King of Delhi."[1] Its object is to examine afresh this document as a test for a theory of the relations between the East India Company and the Mughal Empire, and consequently of the nature of the rise of the British in India.

No theory, it is suggested, has yet given an adequate explanation of the outstanding fact that, between the death of Aurangzēb in 1707 and the outbreak of the year 1857, there was no sign of concerted opposition to the British in India, save the attempts made by Haidar 'Alī and his son Tīpū. And, moreover, that these attempts pro-

duced the opposite effect to the one desired, in that they brought together the Company and the rest of the Mughal Empire.

Further, the intervention of Persia and other northern Muslim powers in the affairs of Delhi during the eighteenth century coincides with some advance of the *Kāfir* against the Mughal Emperor. No intervention appears between the years 1761 and 1857, except the rebellion of Ghulām Qādir in 1788 and the menace of Zamān Shāh ten years later. Both of these appear to have been made at the instigation of Tīpū Sāhib, the anti-*Pādishāh*—to adopt a term used in Papal history—of the Mughal Emperor, Shāh 'Ālam. . . .

In 1857, however, the concerted outbreak occurred, together with the threat of a Persian advance, which was only stopped by the Anglo-Persian War and the pro-British attitude of Afghanistān. The problem then is to discover the reason for the simultaneous appearance of these factors at this point.

[1] An account of the trial is to be found in *Parliamentary Papers*, 1859, vol. 18, Paper 162. [Editor's note]

From F. W. Buckler, "The Political Theory of the Indian Mutiny" in *Transactions of the Royal Historical Society*, Fourth Series, vol. V, 1922, pp. 71–100, selections. Reprinted by permission.

The solution, it is suggested, involves a radical revision of accepted theories of the rise of the British in India. For the last century and a half, Indian history has been represented in Europe almost entirely by the propaganda of the Trading Companies, which approached Indian politics and states under the influence of the Colonial System of Western Expansion. Their much reiterated conclusions have been accepted as axiomatic—even by Indian students—and no effort has been made to examine the biassed judgments of Merchants on the subject of oriental monarchy. In the eighteenth century, it is true, Anquetil Duperron strove hard to secure historical justice for the East, while in England, Verelst . . . strove in vain in a narrower sphere. Later Mill attempted to check the progress of the growing contempt for oriental monarchy, but inaccuracy in detail and antagonism towards Warren Hastings have been allowed to obscure much work that is really valuable. The final blow came in 1835 with the acceptance of Macaulay's Minute on Indian Education, against the advice of the "orientalists," and the consequent victory of the English point of view in the East.

The obliteration of oriental monarchy, its rights, duties, and virtues, by a parade of its vices was not without cause. The East India Company was never really popular in England. To justify its existence, therefore, in the eyes of the British public, it was forced to assume an imperialistic rôle and claim to have acquired territory for the nation. To attain this object, it evolved a fictitious history of India, until, in the first half of the nineteenth century, side by side there existed a politically effective Empire with an accepted history of its non-existence. The Mughal Empire suffered at the hands of the eighteenth century the fate of the Holy Roman Empire.

To account for the rise of the British in India, culminating in the combination in 1857 of the factors already noticed, the theory here suggested is the continuity of the Mughal Empire down to the deposition of Bahādur Shāh II in 1858, as an effective source of political authority and as the suzerain *de jure* of the East India Company in the capacity of *Dīwān* of Bengal, arrogating the title of the British Government in India. In short, that the source of the Company's authority in India lay, not in the Charters of the King of England, nor in the Acts of the British Parliament, nor in the sword, but in the *farmāns* of the Mughal Emperor. That his authority was primarily religious, and political authority fell within the sphere of religious authority. That all honour, claimed by the Company against the Emperor, belonged to the Emperor, its suzerain. That all censure and opprobrium levelled against him recoils on the Company, his disloyal vassal, since his difficulties arose mainly from its intrigues and from the fact that after 1772, the Company withheld and converted to its own use, the revenues of the richest provinces of his Empire.

Secondly, the artificial extension of the Mahratta rebellion beyond the year 1720, by which it was possible to portray as a monster of tyranny Sindia, the only loyal vassal of the year 1788. In consequence, that it was possible for the Company, in the eyes of India, to play the part of a repentant vassal returning to the loyalty of the Mughal Emperor, while in Europe, it posed as the representative of the British Government whose protection it professed to proclaim over the "King of Delhi" and to allege that he had become a "subject" and a "pensioner" of that Government.

Thirdly, that owing to the ignorance of Indian language and conditions, governors-general, who succeeded Wellesley, assumed an attitude and pursued a policy towards the Mughal Emperor which to him could appear in no other light than that of high treason; and the culmination was reached when Dalhousie and Canning attempted to tamper with the succession. From that time it was clear that the over-powerful vassal must be reduced. The army turned to its sovereign's allegiance against its rebel officer. Hence if in 1857 there were any mutineer, it was the East India Company. For the validity of this thesis, it is suggested, the *"Proceedings of the Trial of the King of Delhi"* are the final test.

The ignorance of the Court on the question of the real status of Bahādur Shāh constitutes the main value of the document. Its questions, save on matters of bloodshed, were unintelligent, and its answers are recorded with that fidelity found only in unintelligent witnesses. No hint appears in questions, that it understood the religious nature of his authority. Indeed, the use of the term "Mutiny"—unless wilful, to obscure the issue—is conclusive evidence of that ignorance. Kaye alone of the historians of the outbreak seems to have understood its meaning, which he labours, painfully but vainly, to suppress. . . .

The tradition of English suzerainty over some parts of India—apart from Bombay—was by no means new. . . .

The origin of the tradition is interesting, as it furnishes a striking instance of what was continually happening in European relations with Indian States, namely, mistranslation. It contains in embryo the underlying cause of the "Mutiny."

The servants of the Company in Madras were continually urging the Company to grant them permission to obtain the *farmān,* by which Madras was held, in terms of the English *nation* instead of the English *Company,* so that if the Company broke down all would not be lost. In Persian documents of the period the word *"nation"* is translated by the word *qaum.* This word, however, only denotes the racial aspect of nationality, the political implications it does not touch. The grant, therefore, would be little more than a promise that the *'āmil* of Madras should be an Englishman. . . .

The next stage is marked by the fiction of the independence of the Deccan by which the vassals of the south (*dakhin*) were converted into "native princes." The fiction was repeated in Bengal a few years later. In both cases it arose from a mistranslation (or rather from a confusion) underlying the word *"tribute,"* of two ideas represented by *nazr* and revenue. The word *nazr* was translated into English either as "a present" or as "tribute." Neither word has the exact connotation of the Arabic original. *Nazr,* in reality, means "a vow." The gift is but the symbol of the allegiance offered. *Tribute,* however, is also used of the money due from the *'āmil* whose duty is the collection of revenue. This function is purely economic and the work of an employee. . . .

Similar is the case of Bengal, but there another factor enters as a complication. In 1772, the Company resolved "to stand forth as *Dīwān.*" It did not, however, by that step formally declare the independence of the three *sūbahs,* but decided to carry out corporately and directly the duties undertaken in 1765. . . .

Nazr was offered by the Governor-General, personally or by deputy, until 1843, when Lord Ellenborough "stopped the practice" which, in reality, made Queen Victoria in Eastern estimation at least, hold her possessions as a mere feudatory and vassal of the imperial house of Delhi. In return for the ritual of allegiance, he offered an increase in the Emperor's (so-called) pension. It is clear, then, why "the King was offended with Lord Ellenborough. . . ." He had severed a bond at once religious and political—an oath of allegiance over two centuries old.

The counterpart of *nazr,* the vow, was the bestowal of the robe of honour, called in Persian, the *sarāpā* (*cap-à-pie*) from the manner in which it was worn, and in Arabic, *Khil'at,* from its nature—that it had been worn by the donor. Robes of honour were given by the Mughal Emperor and his deputies to subjects only, in recognition of allegiance (*nazr*) or some act of merit, of authority conferred, of the return to allegiance or of entry into the Mughal State. . . .

From Mildenhall down to Thomason in 1843, robes of honour were accepted at the Court of the Mughal Emperor by representatives of the East India Company.

As with any other vassal or subject, then, a double link of acknowledgment bound the Company in its allegiance to the Mughal Emperor, down to the year 1843 —namely, the offering of *nazr* and the acceptance of the *Khil'at*. Both institutions appear to have a religious significance. Hence it would seem that the source of sovereignty, too, was religious, and the nature of Mughal Sovereignty appears to confirm this view. . . .

In 1803, Wellesley was faced by two issues—one, the possibility of an unofficial French ascendency at the Court of Delhi, the other, the desirability of overthrowing the effective ascendency of Sindia in the Ministry of Shāh 'Ālam. The Napoleonic peril obsessed the minds of all who came from Europe, while plans of a Persian invasion with Bonaparte in alliance increased the apprehension of the Governor-General in India. The news, however, of the diplomacy of the Peace of Amiens and the despatch of General Decaen to establish communication between India and Paris through *l'Ile de France,* forced Wellesley to take such action as would place Delhi outside the range of French enterprise and European International Law. The method he adopted was to avail himself of the possibility of narrowing the connotation of Persian words in translation, and he was able, thereby, to assert *in English,* that he had taken the Mughal Emperor *under the protection of the British Government,* in other words, that he had declared the Mughal Empire to be a British Protectorate.

Whether he could or could not have made the assertion to Shāh 'Ālam does not affect the question. The fact remains that he apparently did *not,* but took advantage of the Company's vassaldom and the vagueness of the Persian language to render his action acceptable to the Emperor and, at the same time, to satisfy the requirements of International Law. In short, he professed to proclaim a protectorate while he merely offered a vassal's protection of his lord. . . .

From the time of Wellesley, the Gover-nor-General neglected to visit the Emperor despite his repeated commands, and though he accepted the *Khil'at,* he refused to wear it. He accepted by touch—but that was sufficient. It was not, however, until the arrival of the Marquess of Hastings, under the influence of the debates of 1812–13, that a more definite assertion of the Governor-General's new position was made. "The Court of Directors [had] claimed the territory of India in the Company's possession as theirs by right of conquest, achieved originally from the profits of their trade: they had paid for it, and it was theirs." Naturally the King in Parliament put an end to such an attitude assumed by his subjects—but, from what has been shown already, it will be clear that the Company was simply playing a double game. The King of England defeated it—Lord Hastings carried that victory to India, also the effects of the Wellesley tradition.

It was necessary for Bengal to break up the Muslim core of the Mughal Empire, and to convert the religious differences of *Sunnī* and *Shī'ah* into political divisions between Delhi and Lucknow. As early as 1775, Warren Hastings had joined with the Nawāb Wazīr against the Court of Delhi by the Treaty of Lucknow. In 1819, the schism was completed by the assumption of the title of *Pādishāh-i-Āwadh* by the Nawāb Wazīr Ghāzī ud dīn Haidar, who struck coin in his own name. The step appears to have excited but little attention in Oudh, where he was still referred to by his Mughal title, as Bishop Heber noticed, but at Delhi feeling ran high.

"The Sovereign of Oude's assumption of the title of King," wrote Hastings, "was treated by the Court of Delhi with undisguised indignation. The offensive animadversions were keenly resented by the Court of Lucknow, and an irreparable breach between these two Mahommedan States is avowed."

The breach, however, was not beyond repair. The ruler of Oudh had placed himself outside the Mughal State. His removal freed Oudh from the stigma of disloyalty, and brought it back within the Mughal Empire—*to the satisfaction of Delhi.* The usurpation by the *Dīwān* of Bengal, however, was resented. It was not the deposition of its King but the annexation that drove Oudh to the support of the Mughal.

Further, Oudh was the main recruiting ground of that portion of the Mughal army which was under the command of the *Dīwān* of Bengal. As the deposition of the "King" of Oudh was followed by similar action against the claims of the Mughal Shāhzāda, threatening the Mughal Empire with extinction, the sepoys clung to the cause of their King and Emperor against the intrigue of their Commanding Officer —the *Dīwān* of Bengal, the East India Company, which, for them, was the mutineer. Of Acts of Parliament they knew nothing, and even if they did, they could carry no weight against the commands of their *Khalīfah.* Not the Court's suggested explanation but this theory I suggest as the true solution to the evidence of Hakīm Ihsān Ullah Khān, who said:

I consider that the native army was impregnated with malevolent intentions towards the British Government; and had even the new cartridges not been issued, they would have made some other pretext to mutiny, because if they had been actuated by religious motives alone they would have given up the service; and if they had wished to serve they would not have mutinied.

But, if the army belonged to the Mughal Pādishāh, and he claimed to be "the divine vice-regent in spiritual matters" . . . the service becomes part of the religious duty— *jihād.*

As has been shown, the Hindus were already alienated by the Company's policy when in some respects it was most Mughal. Nānā Sāhib represented both the Hindu grievance and the unemployed pro-Mughal Mahratta. The issue of greased cartridges merely provided the occasion of the outburst.

The main cause, then, was the treatment of the Emperor. The fiction started by Wellesley was growing more evident to the East. Akbar Shāh was approached with the bribe of an increased "pension" to acknowledge himself as no more than the King of Delhi—he refused, but the fiction persisted in the West. Bahādur Shāh II was approached likewise, and likewise he refused. The next step was so to manœuvre that Bahadur Shah's successor should consent to leave Delhi, for they believed his strength to lie in the associations of the city. . . . This step—of consenting to leave Delhi—was made the price of recognition by the East India Company. Universal recognition may be a condition for the valid election of the *Khalīfah,* [divine vice-regent], but only to the Faithful is the right of dissent. The Company had ceased to belong to the Faithful in the year 1843, so on the 10th July, 1856, when Faqīr-ud-dīn died, the Mughal succession was in a critical state, for the Emperor's most powerful vassal had refused to recognize his son, except on terms tantamount to a betrayal of Faith.

The Company had been warned of the danger when Dalhousie, in 1849, had proposed the removal of the House of Timur from Delhi, but in vain. When Canning, newly arrived in India, was forced to make a decision, he relied on "the minutes of the preceding members of the Government," that is, on the Wellesley tradition, to interpret the situation. His decision was that

To recognize the title of King, and a claim to the external marks of loyalty in a new person, would be an act purely voluntary on the part of the Government of India, and quite uncalled for.

In the events that followed, Canning represented the Wellesley tradition, Zīnat Mahall that of the Persian version of the transactions. The view that mere palace intrigue could have produced such a rising needs no discussion. The cause lay in the conflict of fact and fiction dating at least from the year 1803. The charges against Bahādur Shāh, the authority of the Court to try him and its finding mark the conclusion of the work of the fiction, for a practical element had intervened—the Queen of England as the Protector of her subjects—the servants of the Mughal and his vassal—from the cruelties of a miscarriage of justice, which had involved them in the penalty due to the Company.

British Atrocities

EDWARD J. THOMPSON

One of the conspicuous features of British writing on 1857 had been an emphasis on the atrocities committed by Indians on Europeans. That the British soldiers had sometimes acted with great ferocity was well-known, but the explanation usually given was that they had been maddened by the deeds of the rebels, and that on the whole the British had behaved with remarkable magnanimity toward their enemies.

In a book appropriately entitled *The Other Side of the Medal*, Edward J. Thompson (1886–1946) showed that not only had the British administered ferocious punishments but that several of the worst cases of brutality had preceded such actions by the Indians as the massacre of Cawnpore. Thompson, who was born in India, taught in a college in Bengal before devoting his time to the writing of novels, poems, histories, and biographies. A friend of Gandhi and Nehru, he was concerned at the hostility that he believed existed between the British and the Indians. *The Other Side of the Medal* was intended to explicate one major source of this bitterness.

FREDERICK Cooper, Deputy-Commissioner of Amritsar, wrote a book about [an] exploit which, he believed, would make him eternally famous. That exploit was announced by the Foreign Office in London thus:

The 26th N.I. mutinied at Lahore on the 30th of July, and murdered the commanding officer, Major Spencer; but the mutineers were totally destroyed.

On 13th May the 3800 Indian troops at Lahore were disarmed as a precautionary measure. For nearly three months Sikhs and about 400 Europeans watched them night and day. During a violent duststorm on 30th July there was observed some commotion among them, which British officers afterwards said was panic at the storm.

Whether there had been any preconcerted scheme among the disarmed regiments for a general attempt to escape from their unpleasant position is not known . . . a fanatic, named Prakash Sing, rushed out of his hut, brandishing a sword, and bawling out to his comrades to rise and kill the Feringhees.

He cut down the Major, whereupon the 26th Native Infantry fled under cover of the storm, the few who remained being killed in a furious cannonade which the Sikhs and Europeans put down on their lines. They tried to cross the Ravi next day, but were opposed by some police. Mr. Cooper pursued them from Amritsar, and found this situation:

The villagers were assembled on the bank, flushed with their easy triumph over the mutineers, of whom some 150 had been shot, mobbed backwards into the river, and drowned inevitably; too weakened and famished as they must have been after their forty miles' flight to battle with the flood. The main body had fled upwards, and swam over on pieces of wood, or floated to an island about a mile off from the shore, where they might be

From Edward J. Thompson, *The Other Side of the Medal*. London: The Hogarth Press, 1925, pp. 58–66.

descried crouching like a brood of wild fowl. It remained to capture this body, and having done so, to execute condign punishment at once.

But Mr Cooper was confronted with the difficulty of the man who had to transport across a river a fox, a goose, and a sack of corn. He dare not leave fox and goose or goose and corn together, or either fox or goose alone. He explained the fable to his Sikhs, and the grim practical joke he intended to play on the sepoys, and the Sikhs, he tells us, were immensely diverted with his merry humour. However, everything went well; and his mind, being both pious and poetical, drank in the rich beauty and fitness of the whole scene, recording them afterwards:

Everything natural, artificial, and accidental favoured the attempt and combined to secure the fate of the mutineers. . . . At any moment, had they made an attempt to escape, a bloody struggle must have ensued. But Providence ordered otherwise, and nothing on the side of the pursuing party seemed to go wrong. . . . The sun was setting in golden splendour; and as the doomed men, with joined palms, crowded down to the shore on the approach of the boats, one side of which bristled with about sixty muskets, besides sundry revolvers and pistols—their long shadows were flung far athwart the gleaming waters. In utter despair, forty or fifty dashed into the stream; and the sowars being on the point of taking pot-shots at the heads of the swimmers, orders were given not to fire.

The sepoys, being silly folk, jumped to the conclusion that Mr Cooper intended to give them a trial:

They evidently were possessed of a sudden and insane idea that they were going to be tried by court-martial, after some luxurious refreshment. In consequence of which, thirty-six stalwart sepoys submitted to be bound by a single man, and stocked like slaves into a hold into one of the two boats emptied for the purpose.

By midnight he had 282 prisoners in a bastion at the police-station. There were also "numbers of camp-followers, who were left to be taken care of by the villagers." They pass out of the story, and no inquiry was ever made as to what happened to them. Rain fell, causing the execution to be deferred, but at the same time tinging the scene with a melancholy beauty that was not lost upon Mr Cooper's sensitive and religious mind:

The gracious moon, which came out through the clouds and reflected herself in myriad pools and streams, as if to light the prisoners to their fate.

Next morning a party of Sikhs arrived with a large supply of rope; the rope was not used, as trees were scarce, but the Sikhs enabled Mr Cooper to get rid of his Musalman troopers, whose loyalty, he feared, might not stand the strain of what he intended to do.

The 1st of August was the anniversary of the great Mohammedan sacrificial festival of the Bukra Eed. A capital excuse was thus afforded to permit the Hindoostanee Mussulman horsemen to return to celebrate it at Umritsir while the single Christian, unembarrassed by their presence, and aided by the faithful Seiks, might perform a ceremonial sacrifice of a different nature. . . . As fortune would have it, again favouring audacity, a deep dry well was discovered within one hundred yards of the police-station, and its presence furnished a convenient solution as to the one remaining difficulty which was of sanitary consideration—the disposal of the corpses of the dishonoured soldiers.

The prisoners were pinioned, tied together, and brought out thus, in batches of ten, to be shot. They were filled with astonishment and rage when they learned their fate.

About 150 having been thus executed, one of the executioners swooned away (he was the oldest of the firing-party), and a little respite was allowed. Then proceeding, the number had arrived at 237; when the district officer was informed that the remainder refused to come out of the bastion, where they had been imprisoned temporarily, a few hours before. . . . The doors were opened, and, behold! Unconsciously the tragedy of Hol-

well's Black Hole had been re-enacted. . . .
Forty-five bodies, dead from fright, exhaustion, fatigue, heat, and partial suffocation,
were dragged into light.

These, dead and dying, along with their
murdered comrades, were thrown by the
village sweepers into the well. Cooper continues:

The above account, written by the principal actor in the scene himself, might read
strangely at home: a single Anglo-Saxon, supported by a section of Asiatics, undertaking
so tremendous responsibility, and coldly presiding over so memorable an execution, without
the excitement of battle, or a sense of
individual injury, to imbue the proceedings
with the faintest hue of vindictiveness. The
Governors of the Punjab are of the true
English stamp and mould, and knew that
England expected every man to do his duty,
and that duty done, thanks them warmly for
doing it.

Cooper's *Preface* strikes the same note
—his book, he says, has been written to
show how the Punjab is governed, and
also

that wisdom and that heroism are still but
mere dross before the manifest and wondrous
interposition of Almighty God in the cause
of Christianity.

His book ends:

To those fond of reading signs, we would
point to the solitary golden cross still gleaming aloft on the summit of the Christian
church in Delhi, whole and untouched;
though the ball on which it rests is riddled
with shots deliberately fired by the infidel
populace. The cross symbolically triumphant
over a shattered globe! . . .

It is true that the first claps of enthusiastic approval were succeeded by questioning and disgust, even in India, which at
last so prevailed that his action is passed
over in silence by our histories. But at the
time the approbation for which he confidently looked was forthcoming. John
Lawrence wrote:

LAHORE, *2nd August*, 1857.
MY DEAR COOPER, I congratulate you on
your success against the 26th N.I. You and
your police acted with much energy and spirit,
and deserve well of the State. I trust the fate
of these sepoys will operate as a warning to
others. Every effort should be exerted to glean
up all who are yet at large.

Robert Montgomery, who succeeded
Lawrence as Lieutenant-Governor of the
Punjab, wrote:

Sunday: 9 a.m.
MY DEAR COOPER, All honour for what
you have done; and right well you did it.
There was no hesitation, or delay, or drawing
back. It will be a feather in your cap as long
as you live. . . . The other three regiments
here were very shaky yesterday; but I hardly
think they will now go. I wish they would,
as they are a nuisance; and not a man would
escape if they do.

Montgomery was a leading advocate of
the propagation of Christianity in India. I
do not think it would be possible to comment on his letter adequately. After the
Mutiny he wrote to Lawrence:

It was not policy, or soldiers, or officers, that
saved the Indian Empire to England, and
saved England to India. The Lord our God,
He it was.

A short time after Cooper's exploit he
wrote to Hodson, congratulating him on a
deed which has found hardly any defenders, even among the writers of Mutiny
memoirs:

MY DEAR HODSON, All honour to you (and
to your "Horse") for catching the king and
slaying his sons. I hope you will bag many
more!
In haste, ever yours,
R. MONTGOMERY.

But the story of Cooper's action is not
quite finished. There was one sepoy so
severely wounded that he could not walk
to the place of execution. He was reprieved
for Queen's evidence by "Pickwick" Montgomery's advice:

Get out of the wounded man all you can, and send him to Lahore, that he may himself proclaim what has been done. The people will not otherwise believe it. . . . There will be some stragglers: have them all picked up; and any you get, send us now. You have had slaughter enough. We want a few for the troops here, and also for evidence.

So the wounded prisoner and another forty-one who were "gleaned" from the surrounding country were sent to Lahore, where they were all blown to pieces. In Cooper's words, "the 26th were both accounted for and disposed of." As for his own executions,

"within forty-eight hours of the date of the crime, there fell by the law nearly 500 men." What crime? what law? the reader may ask, demanded the extermination of a helpless multitude, described by the very best authority as unarmed and panic-stricken, famishing with hunger, and exhausted with fatigue?

Greathed remarks:

the sacrifice of five hundred villianous lives for the murder of two English is a retribution that will be remembered.

Yes, it is one of the memories of India,

as Cawnpore is of England. Cooper's narration reaches its climax in these words:

There is a well at Cawnpoor; but there is also one at Ujnalla.

I see no reason why he should be denied the immortality he craved so earnestly. Let his name be remembered with Nana Sahib's. . . .

Sir George W. Forrest's *History of the Indian Mutiny,* which has claims to have superseded Kaye and Malleson's much earlier account as the standard history of the whole episode, manages through three enormous volumes (over fifteen hundred pages) to avoid any reference, however slight and slanting, to excesses or "severities" committed by us. It concludes with an unctuous paragraph on the last three executions, and closes grandly:

Justice was done, mercy shown to all who were not guilty of deliberate murder, the land cleansed of blood.

One might throw the lists open to the literature of the whole world, and still not find a more superb example of smug effrontery.

The Fruits of Capitalism

LESTER HUTCHINSON

Indian history appears to be remarkably free of large-scale peasant revolts of the kind that have provided historians of Europe and China with materials for assessing class antagonisms. For this reason the war of 1857 has been of special interest to writers with a left-wing political bias who wished to demonstrate the workings of the same historical forces in India as they had identified elsewhere. The account given here was written by Lester Hutchinson, an Englishman who was deeply involved in trade union and working class movements in India from 1928 to 1933 and who was jailed for alleged complicity in a revolutionary movement to overthrow the Government. Hutchinson sees the war as the last protest of a feudal order that felt itself inundated by the forces of modernity.

I N A torrent of blood the Great Rebellion came to an end. Hopelessly misled by intriguing and inefficient princes, the people had once again felt the iron hand of a conqueror. All resistance to British rule was now crushed; and there was nothing left for the Indian people except to nurse their bitterness and hatred. The social revolution had been achieved, and a new nation had been created; but it was a nation of slaves, deprived of its historical inheritance.

The British won because great historical forces were behind them; but after their victory they attempted to stem these forces and to arrest all further progress. They ceased to fulfil any social function in India, and their power began to decay. The Great Rebellion marks the end of one epoch in which British imperialism was a progressive revolutionary force in India, and the beginning of another in which the forces of progress are behind the Indian people in their long struggle against a reactionary imperialism, already condemned by history.

The rebellion which broke out in 1857 was neither a military mutiny nor a national war for independence. It was not a mutiny because it was not confined to the troops, but was supported by the vast majority of the peasants and people of northern India; and it was not a national war because as yet there was no nation in India, although the unifying policy of the British was rapidly creating one. It was a revolt precipitated by the revolutionary changes introduced by British capitalism into India, and by the British attempts to break down the feudal isolation of the villages and the States in order to weld India into an economic and political unit under British rule. Historically considered, it was a revolt against nationalism and against modernity: it was an attempt to turn the clock of history back to feudal isolation and to feudal tyranny, to the hand-loom and the spinning-wheel, and to primitive methods of transport and communication.

The Great Rebellion was therefore bound to fail. Although the mass of the outraged people was behind the rebels, history was behind the British (undeserving as they undoubtedly were). The germs

From Lester Hutchinson, *The Empire of the Nabobs*. London: Allen and Unwin, 1937, pp. 136–139. Reprinted by permission.

of failure were apparent in the rebellion from the outset. The leaders, the ruined nobility, could think of no better plan than to declare Bahadur Shah, an old and senile man, but nevertheless the titular Moghul emperor, as the head of the rebellion, of which the object was to restore the old Mohammedan Empire. This move at once antagonized many of the Hindu chiefs, and ensured that the Sikhs, who still remembered the persecutions of Aurangzeb, went over to the side of the British. During the course of the rebellion, Bahadur Shah pottered aimlessly about the palace in Delhi, oblivious to the scheming of his wives and sons and to the quarrelling of the chiefs. There was neither central leadership nor cohesion given to the revolt, which was carried on in a condition of almost complete anarchy, without tactics, discipline, or understanding. That the rebellion lasted as long as it did is no tribute to the leadership, but is a sign of the great popular support given to it.

In the beginning the leadership of the British was almost as bad. When the sepoys mutinied at Meerut, the British officers were paralysed with astonishment and terror, and the garrison of British troops, which might have checked the mutineers, continued their routine drill while the comparatively ill-armed sepoys, having destroyed the gaol and released the convicts, were marching on the road to Delhi. At Delhi the population rose to receive them, and the English garrison, after exploding the magazine, were forced to flee. From Delhi the rebellion raged through the North-West Provinces and Oudh down to Bengal, and many of the princes in Central India threw in their lot with the rebels. In Oudh the feeling against the British was particularly intense, owing to the annexations and to the previous decades of British oppression and spoliation. In Cawnpore, there appeared Nana Sahib, the dispossessed heir of the last Peshwa, who put himself at the head of the rebels and directed the siege of the entrenchments which the British garrison had erected to protect the European population. After a siege of nineteen days, the garrison surrendered on the strength of a safe-conduct to Allahabad offered to them by Nana Sahib, who seems to have been a black-hearted scoundrel even if we make allowances for his grievances against the British. The safe-conduct proved a trick, and the soldiers and their women and children were foully massacred as they embarked in boats on the Ganges. At Lucknow, a relieving force probably saved the garrison from the same fate. . . .

The process of cleaning up took eighteen months. The greatest resistance was made in Oudh, where the rebels were fully supported by the peasants, and in Central India, where Nana Sahib, Tantia Topi, the Rani of Jhansi, and other leaders fought hopelessly but bravely.

The savagery of the repression hardly bears calm comment. It can only be compared with the decimations of Cromwell in Ireland. An attempt was made and is still made to justify this savagery by stories of the frightful atrocities committed by the rebels on British women and children. The massacre of Cawnpore is made the most of in school history books, which incidentally make no mention of the British reprisals. The massacre at Cawnpore was certainly an atrocity which no argument can justify; but it was not committed by the rebel troops who refused to obey Nana Sahib and fire on the unarmed garrison; it was the work of a few personal followers of Nana Sahib. Many Europeans, men, women, and even children, were murdered, and there were doubtless atrocities during the course of the rebellion; but in this connection it is as well to consider Macaulay's explanation of the outrages committed by the people in England two centuries earlier during the Civil War:

The violence of those outrages will always be proportioned to the ferocity and ignorance of the people; and the ferocity and ignorance of the people will be proportioned to the oppression and degradation under which they have been accustomed to live.

The British could hardly expect tenderness from the Indian people whom they had crushed and exploited for more than a century; yet, except for isolated incidents, such tenderness they actually received, from the poor and from the peasants.

There can, however, be no justification for the horrors committed during the repression by the agents of British capitalism, the self-styled civilizers, who, mad with terror and rage, ravaged the country with fire and sword, hanging, impaling, or blowing from guns the innocent and guilty alike. . . .

A Social Revolution

P. C. JOSHI

A modern Marxist interpretation of the war as a social revolution expressive of class antagonisms is given in the following selection by P. C. Joshi, who was Secretary of the Communist Party of India from 1937 to 1945. Noting, as did many students of the period, the apparently important role of religion, Joshi argues that the people were forced to use religious terminology since they were familiar with no other idiom. Like many other modern Indian writers, Joshi regards the war as "the source spring of our national movement," the moment in history when the Indian people in a great upsurge of nationalist sentiment "laid the foundation for the world-wide democratic solidarity . . ."

THE British, under the East India Company's rule, disrupted the whole economic order of India, they turned the traditional land system topsy turvy, they smashed the trades and manufactures of the land and disrupted the relationship between these two sectors of the Indian economy, systematically drained the wealth of our country to their own, and destroyed the very springs of production of our economy. Every class of Indian society suffered at this new spoliator's hands. The landlords were dispossessed and the peasants rendered paupers, the merchant bourgeoisie of India liquidated as an independent class and the artisans and craftsmen deprived of their productive professions. Such unprecedented destruction of a whole economic order and of every class within it could not but produce a great social upheaval and that was the national uprising of 1857. The all-destructive British policy produced a broad popular rebellion against its rule.

Within Indian society, however, those productive forces and classes had not yet grown (in fact early British policy had itself destroyed their first off-shoots) that could lead this revolution to victory. The revolt of 1857 as also its failure were both historical inevitabilities. But it also was a historical necessity, for after it followed those modern developments (which we will later analyse), from which emerged the modern national liberation movement of the Indian people and those new social forces which led it to victory.

The religious factor played a big part in the revolt of 1857. The British statesmen and chroniclers exaggerated and deliberately misinterpreted the role played by this factor to prove their thesis that the 1857 uprising was reactionary, revivalist and directed against the progressive reforms that they were introducing in Indian society. The early generation of English-educated Indian intellectuals swallowed this imperialist thesis uncritically because they themselves had suffered under the old reactionary religious influences. A true historical outlook demands that we do not forget the historical stage which Indian society had reached on the eve of 1857, the ideological values which would be normal to this society and the ideological forms in which the Indian people could formulate their aspirations.

From P. C. Joshi, ed., *Rebellion: 1857*. Bombay: People's Publishing House, 1957, pp. 150–159, selections.

Indian feudal society in the middle of the 19th century was rapidly disintegrating and alien conquerors were seeking to exploit our weaknesses to their own advantage. They were conducting a furious, well planned, economic, political and ideological offensive against our country. The biggest problem facing all classes of the Indian people was to save India for the Indians and defend it from the Firinghis' all-sided onslaughts. In the then historical context, traditional religious-cultural concepts could not but be a very important constituent of the Indian ideological struggle against the foreigner's rule. From his own study of history and people's age-old struggles to remake their destiny, Marx had come to the conclusion:

Men make their own history, but they do not make it just as they please; they do not make it under circumstances chosen by themselves, given and transmitted from the past. The tradition of all the dead generations weighs like a nightmare on the brain of the living. And just when they seem engaged in revolutionising themselves and things, in creating something that has never yet existed, precisely in such periods of revolutionary crisis they anxiously conjure up the spirits of the past to their service and borrow from them names, battle cries and costumes in order to present the new scene of world history in this time-honoured disguise and this borrowed language.

It is not at all true that the British rulers were responsible for the major reforms then introduced, for example, the abolition of *sati,* widow remarriage, etc. For purely political propaganda purposes, the British chroniclers subsequently made this claim. The truth is that the initiative, the popular campaign, etc., for these long-needed reforms came from the Indian reformers themselves.

By the beginning of the 19th century, British rulers had become so arrogant and power-drunk that in administrative methods they wilfully ignored and trampled under foot Indian customs and the mass of Indians concluded that all this was designed

with a view to gradually convert them to Christianity. For example, common messing was introduced in jails. Much more serious was the Act 21 of 1850 which enabled converts to inherit their ancestral property. The reaction produced by this Act and how it made easier the task of converting Indians to Christianity is described by Sir Syed Ahmad Khan in the following words:

The Legislative Council is not free from the charge of having meddled with religious matters. Act 21 of 1850 was without doubt prejudicial to the professors of other creeds. This Act was thought to have been passed with the view of cozening men into Christianity. The Hindu faith, as is known, allows no converts. To the Hindus, therefore, this Act brought no benefit. If a man again becomes a convert to Islam, he is forbidden by the laws of his own religion, from inheriting property left to him by men of another creed. No Mohammadan convert, therefore, could profit by this Act. To such men, however, as became Christians it offered great advantages. Hence this Act was said not only to interfere with people's religion but to hold out strong inducements to conversion.

This interference with traditional forms also invaded the sepoy army. They were banned from using their caste marks, compelled to "cross the seas," go abroad to fight Britain's wars, and most serious of all was the introduction of the greased cartridges. The British commanders and statesmen indignantly denied that any fat or lard objectionable to the Hindus and Muslims had been used. It was subsequently proved that they told a deliberate lie. . . .

The suspicion that the British government was out to Christianise the Indian people was widespread. Let us quote a contemporary Muslim divine's statement. "They left no stone unturned and tried their utmost to bring to an end, the various religions (excepting Christianity) by inventing devices. They established schools in towns and cities in order to teach books of their language and faith to the children and illiterate adults. They wiped out of existence the centres of knowledge and learning and *madrasahs* and institutions which have been established in earlier days."

The suspicions of the Indians were thoroughly justified. The Chairman of the Directors of the East India Company, Mr. Mangles said in the House of Commons in 1857:

Providence has entrusted the extensive empire of Hindustan to England, in order that the banner of Christ should wave triumphant from one end of India to the other. Everyone must exert all his strength that there may be no dilatoriness on any account in continuing in the country the grand work of making India Christian.

*   *   *

The missionary propaganda was not only violently aggressive and widespread but also supported by the government agency. Syed Ahmad Khan states: "In some districts, the missionaries were actually attended by policemen from the station. And then the missionaries did not confine themselves to explain the doctrines of their own books. In violent and unmeasured language, they attacked the followers and the holy places of other creeds; annoying and insulting beyond expression the feelings of those who listen to them. In this way, too, the seeds of discontent were sown deep in the hearts of the people." . . .

The introduction of English education was also not motivated by the pure desire to introduce European science and enlightenment into India but by its very protagonists themselves, directly related to the aim of converting the newly-educated Indians. For example, Macaulay wrote in a letter to his mother on October 12, 1836: "It is my firm belief that if our plan of education is followed up, there would not be a single idolator in Bengal thirty years hence!" . . .

It is abundantly clear, therefore, that the British rulers purely for their imperialist motives were out for some decades preceding 1857 to culturally denationalise India by the method of mass conversion to Christianity. This was seen as a menacing danger by the mass of Indians, irrespective of their viewpoint whether it was Sir Syed Ahmad Khan or Bahadur Shah, whether it was the enlightened Bengali intellectual in Calcutta or the Nana Saheb at Bithoor, by the mass of sepoys both Hindu and Muslim. Thus when the religious factor played a big role as it did in the struggle of 1857, it was as a part of the national factor. The mass of Indians took up arms to defend their own religions and they were fighting not only in defence of their religion but to defend their way of life and their nationhood. Of course, there were several reactionary features within Indian society but then the only healthy way to change them was through the struggle of the Indian people themselves.

This is not all. Our rebel ancestors used religion to advance the revolutionary struggle. They did not let religion stupefy them. . . .

During the siege of Delhi, British agents repeatedly tried to transform the joint Hindu-Muslim struggle into a fratricidal Hindu-Muslim civil war. Even as early as May 1857, British agents began inciting the Muslims against the Hindus in the name of *jihad* and the matter was brought before Bahadur Shah. "The king answered that such a *jihad* was quite impossible, and that such an idea an act of extreme folly, for the majority of the *Purbeah* soldiers were Hindus. Moreover, such an act could create internecine war, and the result would be deplorable. It was fitting that sympathy should exist among all classes. . . . A deputation of Hindu officers arrived to complain of the war against Hindus being preached. The king replied: 'The holy war is against the English; I have forbidden it against the Hindus.' "

Thus did our rebel ancestors use religion to organise and conduct a united revolutionary struggle against foreign domination. In the historic conditions of 1857, the ideological form of the struggle could not but assume religious forms. To expect anything else would be unrealistic and unscientific.

An Episode in India's Freedom Struggle

NANDALAL CHATTERJI

Many academic historians in India, as well as journalists and politicians, have seen 1857 as the year of India's first war of independence and the beginning of the nationalist movement that was climaxed with the winning of freedom in 1947. The centenary of the war witnessed the production of many scholarly articles in the professional history journals arguing that the evidence was such that one was forced to conclude that the war of 1857 must be regarded as a genuine nationalist movement comparable to the European revolts of 1848. (An essential feature of the rereading of the history of the period is the emphasis placed on Hindu-Muslim unity, with the point being made that the two religious communities were moved by a common impulse to create a free India. A contrast is implied with the later period when, because of animosities created by the British, the two groups were unable to unite.) Nandalal Chatterji, Professor of History at the University of Lucknow, summarizes what seems to him to be the evidence for this interpretation in the following passage. Many of his arguments are critically examined in the selections in the next section.

T HE rising of 1857 is Modern India's First War of Independence. It has been looked at and described in various ways. English historians have called it a Sepoy Mutiny, but it was in fact more than a mutiny; for behind the grievances of the sepoy lay a more widespread political discontent among various elements of the country. It is clear therefore, that the Revolt of 1857 was not a simple movement but a complex one. It would be a mistake to treat it as a disconnected and sudden explosion.

The Great Rebellion symbolises a new political awakening in the land. This awakening was cultural, even though the sepoys were one of its chief spearheads. The fact is that the impact of Western civilization had roused the average Indian from his usual complacency and the attacks on religious beliefs and institutions coming from the Christian missionaries had convinced many people that unless India was freed from British rule national culture could not be made safe and secure. But this discontent would not have taken the shape of a widespread revolt, if the yearning for freedom had not stood out as the outward emblem of the decaying old political order of India. *Dharma* or *Din* was the slogan which powerfully appealed to all sections who were disaffected against the foreign rule. Religion and politics became mixed up in 1857 in a manner in which it cannot do so in any other country than India, for the people were by nature and instinct intensely religious.

The real significance of the Revolt of 1857 lies, therefore, in an ideological conflict which took the shape of a patriotic outburst against foreign rule. The rebels had their own grievances. But, how is it that discordant elements managed to combine against the mighty British Empire?

From Nandalal Chatterji, "A Century of India's Freedom Struggle," in the *Journal of Indian History*, vol. 35, Part 2, August 1957, pp. 221–222.

Could individual spite and prejudice have led to a popular revolt? The revolt was scarcely a revolt of discordant elements alone. It is true that the outbreak was not a revolt of the Western type; still it marks a national upsurge for the first time in Modern India. This upsurge was erratic, even isolated, sporadic and unforeseen. This does not detract from the great significance of this upsurge. No revolutionary movement on a large scale can possibly take place only because some leaders are inspired by selfish motives. A widespread conflagration cannot be artificially engineered by self-seekers and manipulators. Such people certainly will exploit the situation favourable to them, but they themselves cannot create the situation. If a national consciousness had not appeared in a vague form the disgruntled leaders would not have been able to create a vast insurrectionary movement. The cartridge affair or any other factor may have hastened the outbreak but was not its cause. The very fact that the rising was not organised by a single group shows that it was a vague sense of political discontent which caused it. Every party took a leap in the dark, conscious only of the fact that they wanted to destroy the British rule. Having begun as a military outburst in various cantonment towns, the revolt assumed in various parts of northern India the character of a popular rebellion.

There are certain things which demand a careful consideration. Firstly, how is it that both Hindus and Muslims joined together against a common foe unless it may be that a common patriotic sentiment inspired them all? Hindu-Muslim unity during the rebellion is a really memorable phenomenon which has so far been completely ignored by European historians. In their common fight against the British the two communities fought shoulder to shoulder. It is a highly significant fact that cowkilling was completely stopped in Delhi during the Revolt. Bahadur Shah's Chief Secretary during the brief period of his restoration was a Hindu, Mukund Ram, just as Nana Saheb's Chief Counseller was a Muslim, Azimullah. This feeling of unity is a symptom which cannot be explained away except in terms of political nationalism.

Secondly, hundreds and thousands lost their all and gave up their lives. Was it because some political adventurer misled them? Thirdly, if the rebels were inspired by the cultural ideology of "Dharma" or "Din," this was the foundation on which Indian national awakening rested in the last century. Fourthly, how is it possible to explain that during the rebellion different elements of society, high and low, baron and peasant, man and woman, Brahman and untouchable, all forgot their differences and joined in a common cause? Fifthly, the fact has not been explained by English historians as to why in various parts of North India the whole countryside was in open revolt. In some areas of Uttar Pradesh even criminals and decoits are known to have joined in a common rising against the British. Lastly, why was not the revolt a localised affair? Even though there was no pre-conceived scheme on a fully national scale, the insurrection occurred simultaneously at many places of the country. Had there not been a common feeling against foreign imperialism the outbreak could not have been widespread. It would have remained a local affair as in the previous cases of the Vellore Mutiny and the Barrackpore Mutiny. A study of the facts would show that the Rising of 1857 failed not because it was not national or patriotic, but because it was not well-organised and well-led.

The Union of the Civil and Military Rebellions

S. B. CHAUDHURI

S. B. Chaudhuri, Professor of History at Presidency College, Calcutta University, has made the civilian disturbances in India in the eighteenth and nineteenth centuries the special subject of his researches. By "disturbances" he means all the varieties of rebellions and insurrections on the part of large numbers of people against constituted authority, as well as the activities of rulers, who, resenting their loss of power, have rebelled against the British. Chaudhuri finds in the events of 1857 resemblances to earlier revolts by peasants against the oppressive system of taxation. He is especially concerned to combat the interpretation of 1857 as the last desperate effort of the old order to maintain its privileges. He insists that the evidence both of 1857 and previous uprisings indicates that the people were conscious that they were fighting for their way of life against an alien aggressor. The landlords who led the revolts in many areas were, he argues, unconscious tools of a nascent nationalism.

THE bifurcation of the subject of the great revolt of 1857 into two distinct historical aspects, the military mutiny and the civil rebellion, has the merit of a new approach and offers the most intelligible clue to a proper understanding and a rational evaluation of the main character of the revolutionary maelstrom. That the sepoys struck the first blow is not denied, that their grievances flowed independently of any external pressure and originated from the conditions of the existing military service also appear quite probable. But their apprehensions and fears about the intentions of the British to destroy their caste and religion were exactly those which troubled the minds of the civil population and the feudal aristocracy as well. This connects the two aspects of the revolt in the historical process. When the sepoys had created the field and attained a certain measure of success, sections of the aristocracy and certain civil elements put themselves at the head of the movement, with the result that the military complexion of the insurrection was changed. The change was bound to take place as the sepoys did not produce a single competent commander who could canalize the activities of the rebellious troops. Naturally enough the initiative and leadership passed into the hands of civilian leaders who turned the movement to their advantage and even led the soldiery to the attack. The sepoys had no plan and resources either, it appears, of carrying on a protracted struggle under their own management, and in many cases they sought the help of the landed dignitaries and even coerced them into leading them if they wavered. After the explosion at Meerut the mutinous troops made for Delhi where resided Bahadur Shah, the emperor according to the Indian legitimists, which gave the movement a traditional countrywide base. The local troops having in a large measure accomplished their plan of overthrowing the British authority in their respective regions proclaimed that the *hukumat* or au-

S. B. Chaudhuri, *Civil Rebellion in the Indian Mutinies.* Calcutta: World Press, 1957, pp. 258–261, 273–299, selections. Reprinted by permission.

thority belonged now to the country chief who had exercised it in the past. . . .

A sense of righteous indignation against the British, whose feelings are so different from those of the Indians and whose gods are so different, must have naturally flowed from the war of the mutinies which gave it the character of a just and righteous revolt, "in reality a great and formidable rebellion," as Disraeli said in the House of Commons. Instead of being a partial military mutiny, a hectic revolt of the Bengal Army alone, the outbreak gradually approached the character of a rising of the people.

The most immediate factor working out this change was the religious element which actuated the masses to sacrifice their lives. The many references to the jehads and the cry of religion in danger which was echoed and re-echoed in the "seditious" proclamations of the period entered into the composition of the upsurge. The extreme ferocity of the mutineers at Meerut and in other places may be explained by the belief of the rebels that they were waging a religious war. . . .

The religious feeling mingled with the racial issue—the universal hatred of the English aliens which gave the revolt of 1857, a national colouring. By no wisdom, by no system, as one contemporary British officer says, could they have prevented the antagonism of race. . . .

The scene of alarm, scarcity and distress presented [throughout North India] brings into prominence the revolutionary character of the objectives of the rebels. It was . . . not a mere wish to humble and humiliate the British government. The total subversion of the British authority in many sectors was only matched by the establishment of a rebel government of a determined character aiming to replace the former rule in all aspects, though many forms were not changed as new ones could not be devised on account of the exigency of the times. Otherwise most of the new government aimed at justice and equality

and embodied to a great degree the spirit of the times. . . .

. . . It however appears quite plausible to maintain that nowhere during this period was any attempt made to establish the principles of democracy and self-government in the administration of the country. Ideas of a free and independent government meant nothing further than the restoration of the power of the local chiefs and were not conceived in the context of the repudiation of the monarchical principle. India in the mid-nineteenth century did not possess the material requisites for advanced political ideas and the insufficiency of her economic life rendered impossible any real extension of the revolution. Nor was there any social servile war, an uprising of the lower against the higher classes.

But this does not mean that the people in general were incapable of social and political initiative. The civil rebellion of the mutinies was mainly a talukdari movement. The movement was a challenge to the British system of law, revenue, production and property relations. It repudiated the British policy of transferring the ownership of land to a new set of proprietors, the auction purchasers and the village headmen. . . .

Yet the rebellion of 1857 was not the work of the dispossessed talukdars alone. The war of the talukdars was made possible only by the co-operation of the general mass of people, the country people, the villagers of different social status. A very singular circumstance which was apparent and worthy of consideration was that the low castes and the cultivators who received attention at the hands of the British government displayed the most marked hostility to it. In Oudh the British were fighting not a mutiny, but the revolt of a people under its hereditary chiefs and leaders. In Budaun the mass of the population rose in a body and the work of rebellion after the sepoys had left, passed into the hands of the rural elements. . . .

In looking at the history of the sepoy

war as a whole, we shall not take a just account of it unless we consider that it was far more than a military and mainly feudal insurrection which it looks like in a first view. The sepoys were no doubt the spearhead of this violent upheaval, but ultimately they fell into the rank of camp followers and swelled the number of feudal levies. The landed chiefs remained in the field almost from the beginning to the end and shaped their activities according to political and economic conditions of their respective localities, but they did not necessarily play a reactionary or conservative part or show any spirit of feudal obscurantism. On the contrary, they became the unconscious tool of a vague feeling of patriotism while combating the anti-feudal tendencies of the British settlement operations.

This is disputed by Dr. R. C. Majumdar. He observes:

The miseries and bloodshed of 1857–58 were not the birth-pang of a freedom movement in India, but the dying groans of an obsolete autocracy. . . .

The whole subject was for the first time discussed in all its bearings in my book, *Civil Disturbances During the British Rule in India* (1765–1857) to which the attention of the readers may now be drawn. Details recorded in that book of the activities of the above leaders will certainly show that they were fighting for their territorial interests in defiance of British authority. Wherever such activities called forth the support of large bodies of common people, as distinct from personal retainers or mercenaries, wherever some initiative in the struggle passed to the inhabitants of the affected area, the historian cannot in fairness deny the existence of a resistance movement, not very far removed from a national movement of some kind. But the whole question is not free from difficulties. A critical perusal of the above book will show that in the pre-mutiny period outbursts of violent types broke out mainly in Bengal, Orissa, Madras, Travancore, Mysore and Malabar—roughly speaking the re-

gion where the mutiny call of 1857 hardly had any response. The leaders referred to in the above list excepting Wazirali came from this belt of country which was the oldest possessions of the English in India. But in the countries which were later on acquired at different stages, that is to say, the whole extent of the sub-continent extending from the Panjab to Bihar and from Dehra Dun to Kolhapur, no formidable anti-British movement originated (excepting those at Bareilly and Benares) in the early period though it was particularly the area where the drama of the revolt of 1857 was enacted. This aspect of the question very forcibly illustrates a line of demarcation which cannot be easily rationalised. Nevertheless, a tentative proposition may be offered in that in 1857 there was the greatest dislike of British authority where it had not yet been long established; and conversely, there was the least effort towards change in those parts of India which had longest been subject to British rule. This explanation does not really cover all the factors which made for the presence, in the new countries and the absence in the old, of the revolt and unrest of 1857. Yet in a way it points to a state of acclimatization and adjustment coupled with the experience of frequent previous suppression that had broken the spirit of many men which prevented the people of the old areas from renewing their offensive in the year 1857. The many sources of discontent and affliction, which were breaking forth in an almost uninterrupted chain of violent current in this area in the pre-mutiny period, did not widen and merge with similar trends of the new areas in 1857. This provided the occasion for the emergence of the northern and the central regions of India into a position of relative importance. . . . In the pre-mutiny period there had not been much combination between the different disaffected elements of the country, the military, aristocracy, priesthood, and commonalty. The sepoy mutinies and the civil commotions had run on two parallel lines. It was the revolt of 1857 which brought about a link-up of all these elements, on a massive scale with a formidable challenge to the alien rule. As such, the 1857 upsurge was undoubtedly national unless we restrict the term unduly.

There is no doubt that the strong undercurrent of popular disaffection which was frequently manifesting itself in open resistance against the British in the early period culminated in the sepoy war of 1857. A few instances of the civil commotion of the mutiny period were really the continuation of earlier outbreaks and some of the leaders of the pre-mutiny period such as Delan Sha, the gond chief of Narsinghpur, Apa Sahib of Nagpur and Chakra Bisayi, the leader of the khonds are also referred to in the official communications of the mutiny period as entertaining hostile designs. The disturbances of the earlier period pointed to a settled disaffection of the people and clearly anticipated their participation in the rebellion of the mutinies. Yet it cannot be denied that the background and the unique situation created by the 1857 mutinies released forces which immensely strengthened the popular uprisings of the sepoy war. The combination and scale of operations stretched out to wide fields and all the elements of discontent and disaffection being focussed in a limited period of two years and not diffused over a century as in the early period gave a new force and direction to the spirit of opposition to British rule in 1857. Viewed in this light the revolt of that year appears to have been the first combined attempt of many classes of people to challenge a foreign power. This is a real, if remote, approach to the freedom movement of India of a later age.

The aristocracy of India was neither dying nor had it yet become obsolete. Though fighting for their lands and rights, the local landed chiefs still could function on a national plane since they brought together an alliance of the diverse people of all classes who made common cause with them in complete disregard of the forces of estrangement which might otherwise exist in the social and economic life. This combination of the local landed chiefs all over the country who were bound by a community of interests, added with the grouping of their followers at cross sections, created possibilities for the foundation of a national front and in consequence united a big portion of India against foreign domination as never before. Thus old feudal instincts and the anti-alien patriotism became mixed up in 1857 in a curious process. The latter was not yet of the pure advanced political type, as the leaven of feudal discontent was still strong. Yet the yearning for freedom which was latent in these instincts stood out as the outward emblem of a national outburst against foreign rule which was rendered intensive by reason of a socio-religious and economic discontent. Here, surely, we have objectively an anticipation of the future and not a mere recoil to the past.

Apparently enough the upsurge appears to have been erratic, isolated from large regions and even sporadic. It was also characterised by lack of efficient organisation on a big scale. But it is no less obvious that the revolt also presents evidence of consistency in so far as the spontaneity of the far-flung movement is concerned. The sepoys starting the conflagration, the British authority superseded, the local leaders setting up independent governments, the landed chiefs reoccupying their estates, and the common people rising in the interior—and all these taking place in utmost regularity, as though in response to a mysterious clarion call, bespeak, at least in a vague and inchoate form, the elements of a national resistance movement against an alien imperial domination.

The want of a concerted plan which was discernible in the rebellious proceedings was inevitable as the rebels though conscious of their object had no precise idea as to the ways and means to be adopted for the destruction of the British power. They took a leap in the dark, people who could not be dreamt of joining the revolt even at the instigation of Mephistopheles were on their feet without thinking of consequences. The movement failed for various reasons, political immaturity, defective military command and indifferent leadership. The excesses committed by the sepoys had also to a great extent alienated the sympathies of the people in many places. Yet it cannot be denied that it was not a movement of the disgruntled elements alone but a rising of the people, at any rate a considerable section of them, who felt, however dimly, the stirring of a common impulse. The character and content of the upsurge that put its stamp on the year 1857 point to a conflict that was larger in significance than that of a mutiny in the barracks. The legacy of a revolution is often laid up in the subconscious mind of the race. It is difficult to trace the causes that work noiselessly to a certain end that is hardly in sight. Who knows that the inception of the nationalist movement was not contained in the rising of 1857 after the fashion of the oak in the acorn? Because the revolt of 1857 was not merely anti-British but a movement expressing profound desires for freedom.

Why the Great Revolt Failed

HIRA LAL GUPTA

Historians who regard the war of 1857 as a nationalist uprising of the people of India against a foreign aggressor are forced to give considerable attention to the reasons for its failure. Given the overwhelming numerical superiority of the Indians, and the supposition that they were fighting for their freedom, the relative ease with which the British reestablished their authority requires explanation. This problem was examined in detail by Professor Hira Lal Gupta of Saugor University in an article in the *Journal of Indian History* published in 1957. Gupta accepts the thesis that the struggle was a war for independence and that Hindus and Muslims worked together in harmony. Unlike earlier historians, he praises the leadership of the revolt for both their courage and their skill. He finds the clue to the failure of the revolutionaries in their lack of technological knowledge and in the superiority of the British communication system.

ALTHOUGH the 19th century political and philosophical concept of nationalism of a strictly western type was not evolved in India till then, the idea of nationhood and the concept of India, as one country inhabited by the Hindus and Muslims, were not new. As compared with the small European countries, India has been a vast sub-continent, equal to more than a score of countries of their size. If, therefore, the Great Revolt of 1857 could not cover the entire sub-continent and some parts remained in a state of smouldering, and could not revolt, due to strong barriers interposed by mountain ranges, difficult travel facilities and language difficulties, or due to strong British position and loyalty of the Indian Princes, and some other parts remained quiet and even supported the British Government, it would be unfair to deprive the uprising of its national character. . . . The dimensions of the rebellion reveal its character as a struggle for freedom. It was presumed with considerable truth that, if Delhi had not been reconquered by the British troops, entire India would have rebelled. To the palpitating hearts of the half-decided, self-interested and calculating people, prone to be on the winning side, the defeat of the British attempts to retake Delhi would have been a signal for a swing in favour of revolt. Help came to the British from several loyal quarters only after Delhi had fallen and the weakness of the revolt was realised. Betrayal and demoralisation among the people came after the tide had turned against the rebels.

With these facts in mind, if Shri Savarkar designated the uprising of 1857 as the first war of Indian Independence, he revealed a simple truth and provided inspiration to the English educated intelligentsia of India coming to the forefront of the nationalist organisations. There is nothing wrong in calling the great Revolt as the national uprising of India against foreign domination. If the limited and unfruitful revolts of 1830 and 1848 in the Central and Southern European countries have been

From Hira Lal Gupta, "The Revolt of 1857 and Its Failure," in the *Journal of Indian History*, vol. 35, December 1957, pp. 345–354.

regarded as national uprisings, there is no reason why the Great Indian Outbreak that convulsed practically the whole of the subcontinent should not be similarly termed. Without the least doubt, the revolt possessed the hall-marks of a truly national uprising.

In this war of national liberation the Hindus and Muslims worked shoulder to shoulder. They harmonised their differences to remove the common yoke. There was perfect cordiality and understanding among them. Its leaders were also drawn from both the communities. There was a large number of local leaders worthy of being remembered as heroes and martyrs for freedom in their respective regions. . . .

Under the inspiring leadership of remarkable persons with granite wills, the war of liberation began well. It spread like an epidemic for the Europeans. Its leaders scored victories everywhere. The British rule was shaken to its foundations. From Delhi to Patna and from Bareilly to the Narbada, British rule was removed from most of the places for varying periods. But the initial success could not be maintained for more than four months at Delhi and for not more than a year at any other place. By the end of 1858, due to the forces beyond the control of the leaders, the revolt completely collapsed, and by 1860 all operations ended. During the period of success as well as defeat the heroism and sacrifices of the revolutionaries were commendable. . . .

The Great Revolt failed in its purpose. Its failure was caused by a number of forces which were simultaneously at work. The revolt was precipitated before it was thoroughly organised and before adequate arrangements could be made for its success. The premature outburst on the 10th of May, instead of a later date fixed for the general uprising (31st of May or 22nd of June, 1857), lacked the well-planned and thoroughly organised strength of a fully co-ordinated scheme. It greatly disturbed the time-table and seriously upset the plan of our leaders. The revolt had to run a great risk of being sporadic in character. There was no dearth of inflammatory material for a country-wide uprising. But, before all the discontented elements could be rallied together to overthrow British rule in the quickest possible time, with the aid and help of the army, so that nothing could be left to chance, the cartridge incident exploded the mine of discontent at an untimely hour. This proved as disastrous to the cause of the revolt as fortunate for the British. . . .

The prematurity of the revolt brought in its train a number of other inevitable defects, which accounted equally for the defeat of the great venture. There was no one master-mind, with military and political foresight, as the supreme head, at whose command the entire revolt could be directed in a planned manner as one movement. It was certain that after the overthrow of the British power an Indian Government was to be established. But what was to be the nature of that government and who were to be the rulers? These questions remained undecided. The north Indian communities had the idea of the restoration of the Mughal rule. The Marathas had the idea of the re-establishment of their domination. This diversity of interests divested the uprising of its strength. Thus, want of centralised leadership, absence of an attractive and captivating ideal and hazy and undecided ideas about the future shape of things to come showed the intrinsic weakness of the Great Upheaval. . . .

The disunity of India destroyed all chances of success. True to the traditions of the subsidiary and tributary alliances, the feudatory Princes not only kept aloof from the tremendous political upsurge, but also rendered memorable services to the Paramount Power, in token of their steadfast loyalty for perpetuating their self-interests. Hardly with any exception, they remained strong bulwarks of the British power instead of making a common cause with the liberators. . . .

All the vested interests in India, whose fortunes were at stake, remained firm in their loyalty. Deeply interested in the continuance of British dominion and quite true to their salt, the zamindars of the areas under the Permanent Settlement, with their control over the masses, showed devotion to the cause of the authors of their fortunes and completely identified themselves with them. Strangely enough, in Bengal, where the pernicious effects of British rule had been felt longer, the rising middle class remained fanatically loyal. No goading could inspire it. At best, some of the upper classes were discussing "which man amongst them was the fittest to be the Chancellor of the Exchequer under the King of Delhi." The Christians, the English-educated people and the Bengalis, Madrasis and Sikhs in the services remained loyal. The Madras sipahis took no part in the storm. On the contrary, they were used for its suppression. . . .

Inadequate military resources of the rebels was the greatest weakness of India struggling for freedom. Apart from soldiers, ex-soldiers and scions of the decaying feudal aristocracy, there was hardly any other section of trained military personnel to fight the war of liberation. With the exception of personal arms and ammunition and those seized from the Government arsenals and magazines, there was no other source from which modern military equipments, arms and accoutrements could be supplied to the people engaged in a deadly struggle. Artillery they had none. The commissariat arrangements were hopelessly insufficient. Besides soldiers, other insurgents fought with their indigenous primitive weapons like swords, spears, sabres, spades and sticks. Without up-to-date war materials, the fight, in the military sense, was between two unequals. Hearts to dare and hands to execute were numerous but the weapons of military warfare were hardly sufficient and efficient to score success over superior military technique, war strategy and discipline and more effective weapons, abundant military resources and inexhaustible supply of reinforcements of all kinds. The much hated Enfield Rifle wrought terrible havoc. The crude and worn-out indigenous weapons and great man-power of India proved to be poor substitutes for it. With better arms and equipment the rebellion would have ended differently. . . .

The financial resources of the revolutionaries were negligible, depleted and impoverished. Like military organisation, their financial organisation also suffered from grievous defects. Finances constitute one of the most important sinews of war. For recruitment, purchase of arms, collection of supplies and maintenance of efficient commissariat, steady flow of money and sound reserves become prerequisites. War entails huge expenditure. Regular supply of money alone could have ensured consistently effective military action. Scanty private resources were undependable. Questionable methods of acquiring money for financing the struggle made the cause unpopular. Captured treasures were not quite sufficient to finance the great venture. On the contrary, the British Government commanded the entire resources of India and, if necessary, huge amounts of money could have been obtained from England. This inadequacy of finances paralysed the freedom struggle.

Modern scientific means of communication under British control, like the widespread telegraph system and postal communications blasted the prospects of success. The revolutionaries did not know their importance and made no concerted efforts to destroy them. The English made extensive use of them for retrieving their position in India. Through them the messages flashed to Calcutta, Bombay and Madras, across thousands of miles, and help could come in the shortest possible time. The copies of the original telegrams hurriedly sent from one place to another confirm the important role of the telegraph system in suppressing the uprisings. From Russell's diary it is known that never since its discovery had the telegraph played so important and daring a role as it did in India during the revolt of 1857. Without it half the British army in India would have become ineffective. The telegraph system served the Governor-General and the Commander-in-Chief better than their right arms. By it they received information in no time and acted with great promptitude. The return of troops from Persia and Crimea was hastened. Reinforcements came from Madras, Burma and Ceylon. The British naval and military expedition on its way to China was intercepted and diverted to India with all possible speed. The march of battalions and movements of artillery and cavalry could be directed telegraphically. Accurate information could be obtained and precise orders could be issued to the generals of the army, stationed in different parts of the country. But for the control of telegraph lines, the quick success of the British would have been more difficult and doubtful, if not impossible. But for it more calamities would have occurred and preventive methods would have become difficult. The telegraph averted uprisings in the Bombay Presidency. It prevented the Kolhapur revolt from spreading elsewhere. It enabled Elphinstone to launch "aggressive defence" as a preventive measure. It prevented the Punjab from catching the conflagration. It was that "accursed string" that strangled the revolt.

The international situation was in favour of the British. The Indian army, which had gone abroad for service, had completed the task assigned to it and was called back without any disadvantage. The Crimean war had ended. Trouble in Persia was over. War in China could be delayed. Had the units of the armies of India and England been engaged in wars in those parts of the world, a very dangerous situation would have arisen for the British in India. The Indian revolutionaries did not know that the armies sent for service abroad would be called back so quickly and reinforcements from England could be possible. Hence, they could not use the international situation to their advantage and thus remained internationally isolated.

The control of the seas, the port towns and the western frontier of India enabled the British Government to suppress the rebellion. The naval power facilitated the regular supply of huge quantities of war material and heavy reinforcements from England. It is said that half of the best of England's army with a large number of highly experienced military officials was sent to India. The control of the sea coast ensured their safe landing. The control of the frontier prevented the turbulent Afghans from taking any advantage of the unsettled conditions in India and joining in the revolt.

The failure of the revolt of 1857 was the defeat of mediaeval ignorance by modern scientific knowledge, of ante-diluvian technique of warfare by modern methods and weapons, of scanty means by superior resources, of weak organisation by a strong one, of inexperience by experience, of mediaeval slowness by modern swift methods, and of indiscipline by discipline. In short, the war of liberation was fought with incomplete plans and a disunited country, scanty resources and unscientific methods and worn-out principles and worn-out arms. These were the well-marked limitations of the Great Uprising. Under these conditions its collapse was inevitable. Unity alone would have been sufficient for political liberation at least for some time. This was the one great lesson which India had to learn from the failure of the Revolt of 1857. Freedom achieved through unity would have been maintained only with up-to-date arms. This is a lesson which our country has to learn to-day when atomic weapons are being piled up on our western border.

PART IV: SUMMING UP

Varieties of Rebellion

HARAPRASAD CHATTOPADHYAYA

Most of the writers represented in this volume would have claimed to have examined their sources objectively and then, without bias in their selection of facts, to have stated their interpretation of these facts warranted. All of them, therefore, could be said to have presented a summary of the evidence. Yet it is obvious that many of the writers sought to make a case, even though they were doubtlessly persuaded of the genuineness of their argument. There are, however, a number of writers who have made a particular effort to examine the conflicting theories and to sum up existing knowledge. Four such accounts are given in this section. The first is by Haraprasad Chattopadhyaya, Professor of History at Asutosh College, Calcutta University. The selection given here is from two different works. In the first part he examines one of the most lively facets of the controversy about the nature of the war: the role of Hindus and Muslims as religious communities. In the second part he argues that no consistent pattern or unity emerges, but that rather one sees a variety of rebellions.

(I)

THE socio-religious policy of the Government of India during the year preceding the Mutiny and the introduction of greased cartridges towards the close of 1856 reacted adversely on both the Hindus and Muslims of the country. When, through the initiative of the sepoys, the Mutiny broke out in 1857, both the Hindus and Muslims joined it in protest against the attitude of Government towards their religious feelings and social prejudices. It is not, however, a fact that all the Hindus and Muslims of the country rose in revolt. As the Mutiny progressed, Government found its supporters among both the communities of the Indian society. Sometimes in the course of the Mutiny they renewed their old feuds and fell foul of each other. But such Hindu-Muslim feuds were sporadic and were confined to certain districts of the then North-western provinces only. Those Hindus and Muslims, who arrayed themselves against Government stood, on the whole, united in common opposition to Government during the Mutiny.

The Mutiny thrived on the disaffection of both the Hindus and Muslims. Both of them had grievances against the British Government before the outbreak of 1857. So far as the Muslims were concerned, they could not forget that not long ago the political destiny of India was in their hands. They still sighed for their lost Empire and longed for its restoration on the ruins of the British power in India. The Muslims of those areas, where Muslim fanaticism ran high, swelled the ranks of the mutineers with political motives. Consequently they came into hostility with the British Government so much so that

From Haraprasad Chattopadhyaya, "The Sepoy Mutiny and the Hindu-Muslim Reaction," in the *Calcutta Review*, Vol. 142, March 1957, pp. 297–306, selections. Reprinted by permission.

they had to suffer much at the hands of the British Government for some years after the sky of India was cleared of the cloud of the Mutiny. In fact, the failure of the revolt was much more disastrous to the Muslims than to the Hindus. The spread of higher education through the medium of English, though much appreciated by the Hindus, did not find favour with the Muslims who had prejudices against learning English. The "mollas" used to forbid it on religious grounds. Status in society then depended much on the knowledge of English. But the aversion of the Muslims to it closed to them every avenue of prosperity in public life and arrested the growth of the Muslim middle-class in the pre-Mutiny days. The eagerness of the Hindus for imbibing western culture, on the other hand, raised their social prestige and decidedly gave them a primacy over the followers of Islam in India. Most of the appointments in the executive and judicial departments of Government were then meant not for the Muslims but for the Hindus, as the latter adapted themselves to the western culture, and the former were loud and strident in their opposition to it. Though the Muslims were thus themselves responsible for being debarred from Government service and for having to face a grave economic hardship consequently, still they entertained ill feeling against Government for their hard economic lot and low status before the Mutiny. The annexation of Oudh in 1856 also wounded their feelings and left them meditating a revenge on the British Government on the eve of the Mutiny. . . .

In spite of the grievances of the Muslims of India against the British Government the Mutiny did not find favour with the entire Muslim community. Muslims from several parts of the country were reported to have openly sympathised with Government during the Mutiny. The Muhammadans of Calcutta reposed their entire faith in the policy of the British Government and pledged themselves to support Government during the crisis of 1857–59. On May 27,

1857, the members of the Muhammadan Association of Calcutta held a special meeting . . . and passed resolutions, expressing their loyalty to Government and promising their entire aid and support to the suppression of the Mutiny. Some of the resolutions, which were passed by them, are cited below:

The meeting having heard of the havoc and devastation, lately committed in some towns of the North-western provinces, and of the sacrifice of life and property, caused by the disaffection and Mutiny of a small portion of the native soldiery of the British Government, do hereby express their sincere regret and heartfelt sorrow at these lamentable and disastrous proceedings.

The Committee learn . . . that the cause of the present Mutiny may be traced to an unfounded report, maliciously spread by ill-disposed men, of a contemplated interference on the part of the Government with the religious rites, ceremonies and persuasions of the natives of this country. . . .

In Southern Bibar the Muhammadans were reputed to be the foremost in acts of devotion to Government. The attitude of the Nizam of Hyderabad towards Government was friendly. While the so-called Bengal Army was carrying fire and sword from one station to another, Hyderabad was in a ferment. Still Hyderabad remained immune from mutinous outbreaks, thanks mainly to the endeavours of the faithful Nizam, Afzul-oo-Dowlah and of his faithful minister, Salar Jung. Wherever in Hyderabad disturbances were apprehended, the Nizam and his minister took prompt action to nip them in the bud. Both of them received thanks from Government in recognition of the services, rendered by them during the disturbances of 1857–58. If the Nizam turned against Government, Southern India would have been in a blaze of insurrection. Again, when the regiments at Chittagong and Dacca mutinied, the Muhammadans of Eastern Bengal treated the mutinous sepoys with much hostility and hunted them out with much pluck.

Surely then, the entire Muhammadan civil population did not rise in revolt in 1857. The Mutiny, in other words, did not thrive on the support of the entire Muslim civil community. . . .

Though a fanatic section of the Muslims of Delhi joined the mutineers, the majority of the Muslim population of the district appeared to have kept aloof from the Mutiny. During the siege of Delhi in May, 1857, the mutineers wanted to have king Bahadur Shah II as their leader. But the titular Padshah was then too old to assume the leadership of the mutineers. The court, that was formed at Delhi under the presidentship of Lieutenant Colonel M. Dawes for the trial of Bahadur Shah, found him guilty not only of open sympathy with the mutineers but also of fomenting sedition by assuming active leadership of the mutineers. But the statement made by the King in the Court in self-defence indicates that he was a prisoner in the hands of the mutineers and that he had no genuine sympathy with them. If he supplied his leadership to the mutineers, he did it most reluctantly.

So, then, the Mutiny should not be ascribed solely to the disaffection of the Muslim community. The entire Muhammadan civil population did not rebel, though many from the Muslim civil society joined the movement; the Muslim mutinous sepoys were numerically inferior to non-Muslim mutinous sepoys; and the Mutiny did not start in the Muslim-dominated areas of the country, as the foregoing paragraphs would show. In the circumstances the Mutiny should not be treated as an exclusively Muhammadan rising on an all-India basis. The Muslim character of the revolt was prominent only in certain parts of the country. In some districts of the North-western provinces, for instance, the Mutiny assumed a Muslim colour. In such districts the hostility of the Muslims towards Government during the Mutiny was quite conspicuous. In Patna also the Muslims stood opposed to Government. . . .

The reaction of the Mutiny on the Hindus may now be studied here. The Hindus also, like the Muslims, had grievances, many and varied, against the Government. The attempt at westernising the Indian society caused much irritation and discontent among the caste-conscious Hindus of the country. The Brahmins and other upper class Hindus stood seething with thousand and one complaints against the governmental encroachment on their sacred domains of caste and prejudices. The spread of English education, systematic policy of Christianising the native population, legal protection, afforded to widows and converts produced a serious Brahmanic reaction in the country. Government was alleged to have violated the sanctity of caste by bringing the highest and the lowest castes together in schools, in the ranks of the Army and in the railway carriages. The sati system was abolished and with it was abolished a source of income of the priestly class. The remarriage of widows was encouraged; the use of common utensils in gaols was insisted on. All such steps proved revolting to the caste-ridden and superstitious Hindu population of the country.

The British Government was looked upon by the Brahmins as a menace to Hinduism, as they believed in the current prophecies that Brahmanism would be abolished and that a new doctrine, namely Christianity would come to prevail. Such prophecies about the end of Brahmanical religion excited among the Hindus the apprehension of a mighty change in religious systems. Among the Brahmins of the pre-Mutiny period there was a superstitious belief that in the existing "kali yuga" all distinctions of caste would be obliterated, and that all men should be of one faith, forsaking the idolatry and worshipping one Supreme Being. Such a superstitious belief cast a gloom on the Hindu society and caused much uneasiness in it. When, however, the Mutiny broke out, it did not find favour with the entire Hindu community. The Hindu inhabitants of the Bhowanipur area in Calcutta remained loyal to Government. On May 23, 1857, a meeting was held by them at the premises of Guru Charan De of the Chakraberia locality of Bhowanipur to consider the best means of maintaining peace in the Bhowanipur area. A committee was formed . . . and the following propositions were carried out:

The Committee being apprehensive of the most deplorable state of things, created by the disaffected sepoys in some parts of the country, consider it as a duty of every loyal subject of Her Majesty's empire to be true to her Government.

As false apprehensions and unfounded tales regarding the exaggerated affairs of Mutiny have prevailed in and about the town through the maliciously disposed persons, the committee feels it as a necessity to remove them from the minds of peaceful subjects.

The committee after mature deliberation comes to the conclusion that some of the members . . . will by every means in their power impress upon the minds of the timid and credulous people the idea of the mightiness of the power of the British Government to repel the aggressions of any foreign enemy, however powerful and indomitable, or to put down any internal disturbance of order.

The committee determine that these noble feelings of loyalty and attachment to the beneficial British rule that had actuated them to meet (here) be most respectfully communicated to the Governor-General in Council.

The inhabitants of the town and district of Barasat in Bengal submitted to the Governor-General in Council an address, in which they recorded their high appreciation of the tolerant attitude of Government towards the people of the country of India, and conveyed their assurance that they would be unsparing in their efforts to maintain order and discipline amongst themselves during the Mutiny. . . .

The entire Hindu community thus refrained from rising in arms in 1857. There is, however, no gainsaying the fact that a large portion of the Hindu society then stood in opposition to Government. The Mutiny, in fact, fattened on the hostility of both the Hindus and Muslims of the country. Though both of them participated in the Mutiny, it was neither the fruit of the conspiracy of the Hindus only nor the result of the hostility of the Muslims exclusively. The Mutiny was a joint movement of both the Hindus and Muslims of the country.

(II)

The nature of the Sepoy Mutiny may now be briefly reviewed thus: In the North-Western provinces, Bundelkhand, Saugor and Narbada had a popular basis. In the rest of the country including the South, the Punjab, Rajputana, Sind, Hyderabad, Bengal, East Bihar, Orissa and Assam, though there were risings of the native soldiery here and there, the civil population remained, on the whole, quiet and peaceful. The Mutiny, in other words, was not a popular movement on an all-India basis. It was popular only region-wise, that is, on a zonal basis. In the regions or zones which witnessed popular risings, the civil population rose in arms against Government not, however, with the political motive of liberating India from the British yoke. In fact, the Mutiny was not a rising of the people for achieving their political freedom. Neither the revolted sepoys nor the rebels from the civil society had the common and positive ideal of realising their political self-determination. The motives with which they were actuated to rise in revolt during the Mutiny were selfish in nature. The Hindus joined the Mutiny in protest against the interference by the Government with their caste and religion. The Muslims also raised the cry of religion being in danger. The dispossessed Muslim ruling class at the same time sought to avail itself of the opportunity to reestablish Muslim sovereignty in India. The dispos-

From Haraprasad Chattopadhyaya, *The Sepoy Mutiny, 1857.* Calcutta: Bookland, 1957, pp. 199–202. Reprinted by permission.

sessed zemindars and talukdars joined the Mutiny to reverse the agrarian decisions of the civil courts and to recover their lands from the auction-purchasers. The villagers, city-rabble and run-away convicts and even many of the sepoys hailed the Mutiny as the most suitable opportunity to plunder treasuries, burn Government buildings and destroy state-records. The sepoys rose in arms to preserve the sanctity of their ancestral caste and religion which were in the danger of being defiled by the introduction of the Enfield Rifle equipped with greased cartridges. Beyond the above-mentioned motives the participants in the Mutiny had no such common political aim in view as India's emancipation from British authority. There were leaders, it is true, at the head of the rebels in different Mutiny-stricken parts of the country but the leaders themselves could not work in harmony with one another in the course of the Mutiny. Neither could they set up an organisation like the Indian National Congress of the later days. An Administrative Court was, of course, set up in Delhi after its capture by the rebels. But this Court was not formed on an all-India basis. Its sessions were held in the Red Fort. Like the members of the Frankfurt Parliament, the members of the Administrative Court had no practical political training and could not, therefore, evolve any policy or programme from the point of view of practical statesmanship. The Court had no achievement to its credit.

Again, the leaders had their activities, if not exclusively, at least largely, confined to their respective areas with the result that the movement failed to have an all-India basis. Kumar Singh, Lakshmi Bai, the Nana Saheb, Maulavi Ahmad Shah and Tantia Topi who are generally honoured as the foremost among the leaders of the Mutiny could not enlist the co-operation of other local leaders like Khan Bahadur Khan, Muhammad Khan and Maulavi Liaqat Ali to work towards a common end. Such leaders as Khan Bahadur Khan, Muhammad Khan and Maulavi Liaqat Ali

often sank into local factions and in some cases pursued anti-Hindu policies, which spelled disaster for the course of the Mutiny. Khan Bahadur Khan, the ruined Nawab of Rohilkhand, entered into a rivalry with another such Nawab of Rohilkhand, Mobarik Shah, both of whom hoped to obtain supremacy on the expulsion of the British. . . . Such a leadership could not command the confidence of the nation at large. Maulavi Liaqat Ali ended his leadership merely by proclaiming himself Governor of Allahabad. Evidently such local leaders were mostly self-centred and only thought of their own immediate gains. They identified themselves with their regional or local interests. They were not inspired by pan-Indianism. Even Rani Lakshmi Bai, Kumar Singh and the Nana Saheb rose in arms out of local and personal grievances against Government.

It is idle, indeed, to plead that the Mutiny was a freedom movement. It may be argued that since the dispossessed Muslim ruling class sought to avail itself of the Sepoy Revolt to overthrow the British Empire in India and to restore in its place the former Mughal Empire with Bahadur Shah at its head, the Revolt should merit to rank as a War of Independence. The argument might have carried sense, if, in the first place, Bahadur Shah had really been in sympathy with the rebels and could be looked upon by all the communities of the country as their rightful representative, and secondly, if the Muslim Government could be treated as the Government of the entire Indian people. But the above assumptions have little to support them. Bahadur Shah had not evinced any genuine sympathy for the rebels. He was never sincerely interested in the cause of the rebels. He played a double game in the course of the Mutiny. Again, to the Muslims, Bahadur Shah, who had kinship with the Great Mughals, might have appeared as the representative of the entire country, but in the eyes of the Hindus and Sikhs he was a leader of the Muslim community only. Both the Hindus and the Sikhs were opposed to the revival of the Muslim Empire in India. It will, therefore, be anything but just to maintain that the attempt of the dispossessed Muslim ruling class to restore the Mughal Empire during the Mutiny lends it the character of a War of Independence.

There is yet another aspect of the Indian Mutiny. Behind the outbreak of the Mutiny in different regions of India the same set of causes had not been equally prominent everywhere. In some regions, the Mutiny broke out for the predominance of certain factors, while in others, it broke out because of the preponderance of other factors. In other words, regional factors predominated over any general or any single common factor in bringing about the Mutiny of 1857. In the North-Western provinces, for instance, the predominant causes of the Mutiny were the resumption of rent-free tenures, auction-sale of estates as a penalty for default under the newly introduced land-revenue system, the play of passions and prejudices of the native people and their apprehension regarding the loss of caste and religion. Again, the fact that North-Western provinces were an important centre of recruitment of the sepoys of the mutinous Bengal Army supplied another predominant cause of the Mutiny in that region. One or other of these predominant causes played its role effectively in hastening the outbreak of the Mutiny in one district or another, in one group of districts or another group in the North-Western provinces. In such districts as Meerut, Allahabad and others, the play of passions and prejudices of the native people and their apprehension regarding the loss of caste and religion mainly caused the Mutiny. In the Revolt in such districts as Budaun, Saharanpur, and Muzaffarnagar, the resentment for the land-revenue policy of Government found a prominent expression. In Moradabad, Bareilly, Budaun, Bijnor, and Shahjahanpur, the hostility of the Muslim community towards Government was conspicuous during the Mutiny. In Delhi also a fanatic section of the Muslims stood aggressive during the Mutiny. In the Saugor and Narbada territories, the apprehension regarding the loss of caste and religion and the application of the Thomasonian principles to the land-revenue settlement were the predominant causes of the Mutiny. In Jhansi, the fact of annexation and the alarm, produced by the rumour that Government was seeking to invade the sacred domains of the native caste and religion, made the civil and military classes rebellious. The Rani was also ultimately forced by circumstances to throw herself into the thick of the struggle with Government to fight out her own cause. After a display of unique heroism she embraced death on the battle-field. Again, the revolt in Oudh was due to such principal causes as its annexation by Lord Dalhousie, introduction of a revenue-system, which abolished the rank of talukdars, and the disbandment of the native Army of the deposed Nawab. Again, Oudh was the nursery of the Bengal Army. The revolt of the Bengal Army naturally also paved the way for the outbreak of revolt in Oudh. . . .

To conclude, the Sepoy Mutiny, as the foregoing analysis shows, did not find favour with the entire civil population of the country. The entire native Army had not revolted and the majority of the landed and territorial aristocrats of the country were then favourably disposed towards the British Government. The so-called leaders of the Mutiny could set up no such central organisation with a clear-cut, commonly accepted and positive political programme as the Indian National Congress of the later days. How can, then, the Sepoy Mutiny be treated as a national or freedom movement? It was, no doubt, a popular movement on a regional basis. But a popular movement is not necessarily a national or freedom movement. People of a country may support a movement on grounds other than political. Such a movement *sans* political basis is not national, though it is popular in character. A freedom movement has a positive political ideal to attain, the ideal of building up a free and sovereign state. The movement of 1857 had no such political ideal before it. The leaders of a freedom movement instill into the minds of the people they lead decisive political doctrines, equip them with phrases, formulas and arguments and give their mind a revolutionary tone and cast. They destroy the prevailing regime but have at the same time a constructive programme to follow after the independence is achieved. They establish a centralised state to which common allegiance of the people is demanded, provide them with an organisation of revolutionary activities. The leaders also seek to arouse the people to their national consciousness, to the sense of their ethnological, linguistic and cultural unity in the course of the freedom movement. The leaders of the Sepoy Mutiny had no such political part to play, no such political missions to fulfil. There was then no Jefferson or Mazzini to inspire the Indian people with the ideal of fighting for freeing their country from the British control, to stamp them with oneness of political feeling and to make them conscious of their unity in the midst of diversity. They could establish no such central organisation as could claim common allegiance of the people of the country. Their motives, above all, were selfish and their interests, local. The people also were actuated, in their opposition to the established authorities, by their selfish and particular motives. The Sepoy Mutiny thus lacks the characteristics of a freedom movement. The end of the Mutiny did not see India freed from the British yoke. Rather it saw the completion of the work initiated by the battles of Plassey and Buxur.

The Inevitability of the Mutiny

S. N. SEN

What may be described as the "official" history of the war of 1857 is the product of one of India's most distinguished educators, Surendra Nath Sen, formerly Head of the Department of History, Calcutta University, and Vice-Chancellor of Delhi University from 1950 to 1953. Although commissioned by the Government of India less than ten years after India had won her independence, and despite what must have been strong pressures to present the war of 1857 as a nationalist struggle, the book is remarkably judicious and free from rancor. Sen shows how conflicting much of the evidence is, and makes clear that it cannot be characterized as a great nationalist uprising. It was rather, he argues, the almost inevitable consequence of a system where the rulers and the ruled shared no common ties of history, race, language, or religion, and yet where the power of enforcing control was to a remarkable extent in the hands of Indian soldiers who had no reason to be loyal to the British.

W E HAVE seen how the movement of 1857 originated, gained in momentum, and ran its course. Was it a spontaneous outburst of sepoy discontent or a premeditated revolt engineered by clever politicians? Was it a mutiny limited to the army or did it command the support of the people at large? Was it a religious war against Christians or a racial struggle for supremacy between the black and the white? Were moral issues involved in this mutiny and did the combatants unconsciously fight for their respective civilisation and culture? These are some of the questions that must be answered fairly and squarely.

The story of the chapatis lends some colour to the theory of prior preparation, propaganda, and conspiracy. In January 1857 small wheaten cakes were circulated from village to village in many districts of Northern India. A sinister meaning was later read into it but it is doubtful whether the mysterious cake bore any evil portent. District officers were naturally interested and made some enquiries. . . . Wallace Dunlop of Meerut says that the chaukidars were under the impression that the cakes were distributed by order of the Government. "The transmission of such little cakes from one district to another is supposed by the Hindoos to effect the removal of epidemic disease." . . . Sir Syed Ahmed points out that cholera was prevalent at the time of the circulation of chapati which was according to some people a talisman to ward off the disease. "The fact is that even at the present day we do not know what caused the distribution of those chuppaties." A conspiracy is not conducted through such an unintelligible and uncertain medium of communication when it did not demand much ingenuity to find a more effective device. The Government would not have failed to discover some evidence if chapatis had a political motive behind them. . . .

Nor were the sepoys or their leaders in league with any foreign power. There is no evidence whatever that the Mutiny was

From S. N. Sen, *Eighteen Fifty-Seven*. New Delhi: The Publications Division, Ministry of Information and Broadcasting, the Government of India, 1957, pp. 398–418, selections.

inspired by Russia. In the King's trial it was alleged that he had sent envoys to Persia. The Persians would doubtless have been glad to foment troubles in India when they were at war with England. A proclamation purporting to come from the Shah, it is true, was once displayed at the Jami Masjid, but it was promptly removed and went unnoticed by the general public of Delhi. In so large a country individuals were not wanting who felt the humiliation of the foreign rule, and the paper in question must have come from one of them. . . .

The only foreign power that the rebels ever approached was Nepal and that was after and not before the Mutiny. That fairly disposes of the first question. The movement of 1857 was not pre-planned, it was not engineered by any political party in India or any foreign power hostile to England. It had its origin in sepoy discontent and derived its strength from the widespread disaffection among the civil population. The bulk of the army came to harm by the persistent policy of rendering them harmless. . . .

The movement drew its recruits from many sources. The Chartists in England had in their ranks the currency reformers and other elements that did not subscribe to their political creed. Diverse parties professing diverse views are apt to join hands against the constituted authorities of a state, once active discontent finds an organised channel of expression. The same thing happened in India in 1857. The movement began as a military mutiny but it was not everywhere confined to the army. It should be noted that the army as a whole did not join the revolt but a considerable section actively fought on the side of the Government. Its actual strength is not easy to compute. Every disarmed regiment was not necessarily disloyal and every deserter was not a mutineer. The fidelity of the 4th N.I. at Kangra and Nurpur was never suspected, and the sepoys, disarmed at Agra, were afterwards recalled to service at the instance of Outram. . . .

Care should be taken not to confuse cause with effect and revolt with anarchy. A law-breaker was not necessarily a patriot. When the administration collapsed the lawless elements once more took the upper hand. The Gujars robbed both sides with equal impartiality though they were not interested in the politics of the day. Old feuds were revived and one village fought another, irrespective of their political alignment. The rural area witnessed many minor incidents which were only the offshoots of the main movement but did not contribute to its strength . . . There was the strange case of Devi Singh in the district of Mathura . . . [who] proclaimed himself the "King of Fourteen Villages," under the impression that British rule had come to an end. When [the District Officer] went to arrest the rebel chief he discovered that the redoubtable Raja was an ordinary rustic incapable of doing much harm. . . .

In Oudh, however, the revolt assumed a national dimension though the term must be used in a limited sense, for the conception of Indian nationality was yet in embryo. To the Punjabi the Hindustani was still a stranger, very few Bengalees realised that they belonged to the same nation as men from Maharashtra and the people of Central India and Rajputana did not acknowledge any bond of kinship with the people of the South. The unity of a common bondage had, however, ushered in a vague sense of a different kind of unity, though the idea had not yet taken root in the society in general. But in spite of racial, religious, and linguistic differences the people of India felt that they had something in common as against the Englishmen. That is why a Rajput bard found in the Jat victory at Bharatpur a theme worthy of his muse, and the Bundela delighted in the British disaster in Nepal. Religion is the most potent force in the absence of territorial patriotism and in 1857 men from all walks of life joined hands with the sepoys in the defence of religion. The feudal lords of Oudh summoned their tenants not only in the name of religion but also in the name of their king. Their king had been unjustly deposed, their country forcibly annexed, and they had not only a political grievance to redress but a moral wrong to undo. . . .

The patriots of Oudh fought for their king and country but they were not champions of freedom, for they had no conception of individual liberty. On the contrary they would, if they could, revive the old order and perpetuate everything it stood for. The English Government had imperceptibly effected a social revolution. They had removed some of the disabilities of women, they had tried to establish the equality of men in the eye of law, they had attempted to improve the lot of the peasant and the serf. The Mutiny leaders would have set the clock back, they would have done away with the new reforms, with the new order, and gone back to the good old days when a commoner could not expect equal justice with the noble, when the tenants were at the mercy of the talukdars, and when theft was punished with mutilation. In short, they wanted a counter-revolution. Whether military success would have ensured it, is another question.

Nor was it a war between the white and the black. All the whites in India were indeed ranged on one side irrespective of their country of origin, but not the black. As Medley points out, "In fact (counting the camp followers), for every white man in camp there were certainly twenty black ones." And but for the camp-followers the white troops would have been ineffective. It was the Indian cook who brought the white soldier his dinner under the heaviest fire, it was the Indian bhisti who brought him his drink in the thickest of the fight, it was the Indian dooly-bearer who carried the wounded out of the danger zone and the Indian servant who looked after his general comfort. But, even if the non-combatants are left out of account, there was a high proportion of Indian soldiers in the army that suppressed the Mutiny. Of 11,-200 effective troops before Delhi no less than seven thousand nine hundred were Indians. It was, therefore, a war between the black insurgents and the white rulers

supported by other blacks. It was the case of one slave rivetting the fetters of another under the supervision of their common master.

No moral issues were involved in the war of 1857. As in other wars, truth became the first casualty and both sides were guilty of false propaganda. At this distance of time it is not possible to ascertain whether this was deliberately done or the parties responsible were honestly convinced that their information was correct. The struggle may be characterised, as Rees has done, as "a war of fanatic religionists against Christians" but during the Mutiny the moral principle underlying their respective religions had little influence on the combatants. The Scriptures were quoted in palliation of transgressions by both the belligerents. Christians had won but not Christianity. The Hindus and Muslims were worsted but not their respective faiths. Christianity like Western science influenced the Indian mind but the missionary had no notable success in his work of proselytisation.

Nor was the war of 1857 a conflict between barbarism and civilisation, for neither side observed a single restriction which humanity had imposed and which oriental and occidental nations had tacitly agreed to honour. It was an inhuman fight between people driven insane by hatred and fear. The non-combatants suffered as badly at the hands of infuriated soldiery as the man in arms; age and sex offered scanty protection against primitive cruelty, and even death brought no immunity from wanton insult. To revive the memory of those evil days may not be desirable but history must record how war debases human character, how thin is the mask of civilisation we wear, how readily the dormant passions are awakened and the Hindu, Muslim, and the Christian alike relapse into the primitive savagery from which religion and civilisation had apparently reclaimed their remote ancestors. . . .

The Mutiny was inevitable. No dependent nation can for ever reconcile itself to foreign domination. A despotic government must ultimately rule by the sword though it might be sheathed in velvet. In India the sword was apparently in the custody of the Sepoy Army. Between the sepoy and his foreign master there was no common tie of race, language, and religion. The Indian could not possibly feel that loyalty for the British crown which the Englishman imbibes with his mother's milk. The traditional obligation of salt had so long held the sepoy and his employers together but it was no substitute for loyalty and patriotism. The sepoy enlisted for the sake of his bread and sooner or later he was bound to recoil against the obvious humiliation of his unnatural position, for as a sepoy it was his duty to hold his country under the foreign heel. He probably did not think in such clear terms but he suffered from a sense of inequality which he could not ignore, for a foreign government may hold the scales even between one individual of the conquered community and another but it cannot be fair to the subject race as against the ruling nation. The Mutiny was not inevitable in 1857 but it was inherent in the constitution of the empire. . . .

The educated Indian at first had no faith in armed rebellion, and the failure of the revolt confirmed him in his conviction. He placed his hope in British liberalism and he had no doubt that as soon as he proved himself worthy of it, the countrymen of Hampden, Milton, and Burke would restore to him his birthright. But hope deferred made his heart sick and his faith wavered, and a new generation arose who had more confidence in the violent methods of the Italian Carbonari and the Russian Nihilist than in the discredited method of constitutional agitation. He was also inspired by the memory of the Mutiny and during the two World Wars the Indian revolutionaries did not relax in their efforts to organise another military rising. The British Government in India became more and more convinced that in their political struggle with Nationalist India they could not entirely depend upon the army. The non-violent non-cooperation movement of Mahatma Gandhi converted the country to a new philosophy and dealt a further blow at the British bureaucracy in India. England retired from India with good grace and undiminished prestige. India has achieved more than the independence for which the heroes of 1857 fought. She has achieved freedom and liberty.

The Absence of Nationalism

R. C. MAJUMDAR

In the preface to the book from which the following selection is taken, R. C. Majumdar comments that it may seem strange that having devoted a long scholarly life to the study of ancient India that he should have undertaken "at the fag end of (his) life to have written a history of the Sepoy Mutiny of 1857." Acknowledged as one of the greatest of Indian historians, Majumdar has held many high posts, including the Vice-Chancellorship of Dacca University. He was instrumental in having the Government of India sponsor the writing of a history of the freedom movement, and, because of this, was asked to prepare the initial study on the war of 1857. After beginning the work, he discovered, in his own words, that he was expected to show that "in 1857 an organized attempt was made by the natural leaders of India to combine themselves into a single command with the sole object of driving out the British power from India in order that a single, unified politically free and sovereign state [might] be established." Majumdar felt that he could not collect and edit his materials to fit a preconceived solution and resigned from the Board that was responsible for the history. He then wrote, and published privately, his own account of 1857. He found nothing in the evidence to suggest that the leaders, particularly Nana Sahib and the Rani of Jhansi, were motivated by nationalist sentiments; their involvement can be understood, he insists, by reference to personal grievances and self-interest. While he asserts that there is an absence of nationalism in 1857, he points out that the revolt had significance for the later, and genuinely nationalistic, movements of the twentieth century.

1. THE EXTENT OF REBELLION

It would appear . . . that the great outbreak of 1857 assumed different aspects in different areas. In some places it was purely a mutiny of the sepoys, joined at a later stage by some discontented elements as well as the riff-raff and other disturbing elements of society who are always eager to take advantage of anarchy and confusion to serve their own ends. In other areas the Mutiny was succeeded by a general revolt in which, in addition to the above elements, other classes of people, particularly dispossessed chiefs, ejected landlords and tenants, and other persons nourishing personal grievances joined in the fray in the hope of regaining their power and possessions. In addition to these two we may note a third area in which we can trace a sullen discontent against the British and passive, even active, sympathy with the mutineers among the civil population or certain sections of it, but no overt acts of rebellion by them.

If we now proceed to make a geographical distribution of those three areas we have to include the Panjab and a large part of Madhya Pradesh under the first zone; the greater part of U.P., a small part of Madhya Pradesh and the western part of Bihar under the second zone; and nearly the whole of Rajasthan and Maharashtra under the third zone. In spite of petty local risings here and there, the whole of Bengal, Assam, Eastern Bihar, Orissa, Eastern Deccan and South India practically remained unaffected by the great outbreak.

As regards the second zone, where alone

From R. C. Majumdar, *The Sepoy Mutiny and the Revolt of 1857*. Calcutta: Mukhopadhyay, 1957, pp. 224–39, selections. Reprinted by permission.

the revolt seemed to be of a popular or national character, there were particular local reasons for it, at least in respect of Avadh, which was so arbitrarily annexed only a year before the Mutiny broke out. As we shall see later, many have regarded this act on the part of Dalhousie as one of the chief and immediate causes of the Mutiny. Even the British authorities in England had to admit the special reasons for violent outbreak in Avadh, as is shown by the following extract from a letter written by the Secret Committee of the Court of Directors to the Governor-General on 19 April, 1858.

War in Oudh has derived much of its popular character from the sudden dethronement of the Crown and the summary settlement of the revenue which deprived a large number of landlords of their lands.

Under the circumstances, hostilities which have been carried on in Oude have rather the character of legitimate war than that of rebellion.

As noted above, a regular government was set up at Lakhnau under the son of the ex-King Wajid Ali, but the real powers behind the throne were the Begum and Ahmadulla.

If we turn to the other prominent leaders associated with the movement, namely Bahadur Shah, Nana Sahib, the Rani of Jhansi, and Kunwar Singh, it immediately strikes us that all these four were smarting under grievous injury done to them by the British and, therefore, bore special grudge against them. It may be argued that although they were actuated primarily by self-interest they might at the same time have been inspired by the idea of patriotism. This may be so, for all we know, but we have no evidence in support of it. It is an undeniable fact that all the leading figures in this great outbreak were alienated from the British for private reasons. It may be a pure accident, but the fact remains.

It is often urged that they were the natural leaders under whom the Indians fought the War of Independence. It is not easy to understand in what sense these four

persons could be regarded as natural leaders. The first was a dotard and a puppet on the throne of the Mughals, who inherited nothing but their name, and had little power and less knowledge of men and things. The second was an adopted child of a worthless wicked ex-Peshwa who was mainly instrumental in ruining the Maratha power. These have certainly no better claim to be regarded as natural leaders than the hundreds of ruling chiefs in India, and in particular the more eminent among them such as the Sindhia, the Holkar, the Nizam and the various Rajput chiefs. Neither the Rani of Jhansi nor Kunwar Singh, in spite of their personal ability, has any right to be called a natural leader of the country. The first was the young widow of an almost unknown ruler of a petty State, then defunct, and the second was a small Talukdar in the interior of Bihar, utterly impoverished beyond hopes of recovery. Even their names were probably unknown before 1857 to persons beyond a hundred miles of their native places. . . .

2. COMMUNAL RELATIONS

Those who look upon the outbreak of 1857 as a national revolt advance as a strong argument in support of their view that it was a joint endeavour of the two great communities, *viz.* Hindus and Mussulmans. But though the sepoys and the common people of both the communities fought together against the English, we miss that real communal amity which characterises a national effort. It is a significant fact that the contemporary Englishmen generally viewed the outbreak mainly as the handiwork of the Muslims. Reference may be made to a few opinions out of many. Thus Raikes says: "They (the Muslims) have behaved in the part of India where I had jurisdiction, very ill; so ill indeed, that if the rest of the population had sympathised with them, instead of antagonised, I should despair of governing India for the future." . . .

Raikes is supported by other contemporary Englishmen. Roberts (later Field-Marshal) wrote that he would "show these rascally Musalmans that, with God's help, Englishmen will still be masters of India." Mrs. Coopland writes: "As this is completely a Mahomedan rising, there is not much to be feared from the Hindoos of Benares." Captain P. G. Scot remarks in his Report on the mutiny at Jhansi: "At Nowgong and Jhansi they let the infantry begin the mutiny. I believe the reason was solely that they wished to conceal the character of the movement, *viz.* its being a Mahomedan one. They were the most blood-thirsty, when the mutiny did break out."

Even Sir Syed Ahmad indirectly admitted the fact when he said: "The Muslims were in every respect more dissatisfied than the Hindus, and hence in most districts they were comparatively more rebellious, though the latter were not wanting in this respect."

Not only the Europeans, but even the Muslims themselves, at least a section of them, believed that they were the senior partners in the great undertaking. This is quite clear from the many Proclamations issued by the Muslim chiefs who had assumed independent authority in various localities. Reference may be made to the two Proclamations issued by Khan Bahadur Khan of Bareilly whose activities have been described above. Throughout his Proclamations runs the assumption that while the Muslims are exerting themselves to the utmost, the Hindus are lukewarm in their efforts. Accordingly a bait was offered to the Hindus. "If the Hindoos," so runs the Proclamation, "shall exert themselves in the murder of these infidels and expel them from the country, they shall be rewarded for their patriotism by the extinction of the practice of the slaughter of the kine." But it was made abundantly clear that "the entire prohibition of this practice is made conditional upon the complete extermination of the infidels from India. If any Hindoo shall shrink from joining in this cause, the evils of revival of this practice shall recoil upon them."

It is also a very significant fact that all the Proclamations of the Muslim chiefs in Avadh and Rohilkhand contain an appeal to the Muslims in the name of their religion, and remind them on their faith in the Quran, that by fighting against the infidels, or paying money to others to fight, they would secure to themselves eternal beatitude. To the Hindus also the appeal was made in the name of their religion by pointing out how the British Government defiled it by introducing the remarriage of widows, the abolition of Suttee, etc. To the native rulers also, after referring to the annexation of states, appeal was made in the name of religion. "Their designs for destroying your religion, O Rajas, is manifest. . . . Be it known to all of you, that if these English are permitted to remain in India, they will butcher you all and put an end to your religion."

It is quite obvious that the idea of a common national endeavour to free the country from the yoke of the British is conspicuous by its absence in these Proclamations. Indeed we could hardly expect such an idea in those days from people of this class, though in our national enthusiasm in later days we attributed it to them.

It is equally obvious that the great difference between the Hindus and the Muslims loomed large even in the territories where the revolt of the civil population was most widely spread. An attempt was made to minimise the evil by emphasising the paramount need of unity between the two communities. A Proclamation was issued at Delhi with the royal permission, urging the two communities to unite in the struggle. But it also stressed the religion as the guiding force of the movement. In view of its importance it may be quoted in full:

To all Hindoos and Mussulmans, citizens and servants of Hindostan, the Officers of the Army now at Delhi and Meerut send greeting:

It is well known that in these days all the English have entertained these evil designs— first, to destroy the religion of the whole Hindustani Army, and then to make the people by compulsion Christians. Therefore we, solely on account of our religion, have combined with the people, and have not spared alive one infidel, and have re-established the Delhi dynasty on these terms. Hundreds of guns and a large amount of treasure have fallen into our hands; therefore, it is fitting that whoever of the soldiers and people dislike turning Christians should unite with one heart, and, acting courageously, not leave the seed of these infidels remaining.

It is further necessary that all Hindoos and Mussulmans unite in this struggle, and, following the instructions of some respectable people, keep themselves secure, so that good order may be maintained, the poorer classes kept contented, and they themselves be exalted to rank and dignity.

But the communal spirit was too deeply rooted to be wiped out by mere pious wishes embodied in Proclamations, even of the King himself. It raised its ugly head in the city of Delhi itself even when its siege by the British was imminent, and the fate of the whole struggle depended upon its successful defence by the combined efforts of all communities. Thus we read in Jiwanlal's Diary, under the date, May 19: "This day the standard of the Holy War was raised by the Mahommedans in the Jumma Masjid. The people of Dharampur and the low characters of the city were concerned in this act. The King was angry and remonstrated, because such a display of fanaticism would only tend to exasperate the Hindus.". . .

But the communal spirit was not confined to Delhi. We learn from official report that on the night of the mutiny (June, 4) at Varanasi "news was received that some Mussulmans had determined to raise the Green Flag in the temple of Bishessur . . . Mr. Lind called on the Rajputs in the city to prevent the insult to their faith. So the Mussulmans retired peacefully."

The communal hatred led to ugly communal riots in many parts of U.P. [the United Provinces]. Green Flag was hoisted and bloody wars were fought between the Hindus and Muslims in Bareilly, Bijnor, Moradabad and other places where the Muslims shouted for the revival of the Muslim kingdom.

Such communal ideas persisted even long after the Mutiny. Blunt, an eminent Englishman, who visited India during the Viceroyalty of Lord Ripon, was told by an old Muslim Grandee, the Chief of Loharo, more than twenty years later, that "what he did not like about the Mutiny was that most of them were Hindus." Such communal feelings were not, of course, universal, but it is clearly proved by the Proclamations and Hindu-Muslim riots that they largely prevailed in U. P., the only province in which the outbreak developed into a general revolt. Even the mass revolt in U. P. can, therefore, be scarcely regarded as a national war of independence.

The communal feeling was not the only obstacle to the solidarity of a national spirit. There was racial animosity produced by historical causes. It was most clearly manifested in the suspicion and jealousy, if not positive hatred, between the Muslims on the one hand and the Marathas and the Sikhs on the other. The British statesmen in India were fully cognisant of this and exploited it to their advantage. As a concrete instance reference may be made to the situation in Hyderabad in 1857, where anti-British feeling was roused by the events in Northern India, and the elements of insurrection were as rife as in many other parts where it actually broke out. . . .

This racial feeling was certainly shared by the Sikhs. The proclamation of Bahadur Shah as Emperor alienated them as they naturally interpreted it as the restoration of the rule of the Muslims from whom they had suffered so much in the past. It is on record that high British officials in the Panjab successfully persuaded the Sikhs to cast in their lot with them by describing in vivid language the injuries and insults they had suffered in the past in the hands of the Mughal Emperors. Having impressed this point on their mind they held out before them the grand opportunity they now had of taking full vengeance. There can be hardly any doubt that the Sikhs were largely influenced by such considerations in wholeheartedly offering their services to the British Government.

There are good grounds to believe that the same spirit alienated the Rajputs and the Marathas, as they, too, for historical reasons, did not favour the restoration of the Muslim rule. This view is supported by the conduct of Nana Sahib, first in inducing the sepoys not to proceed to Delhi, and then in proclaiming himself as the Peshwa. It is also to be noted that none of the Rajput and Maratha chiefs responded to the invitation of Bahadur Shah, and all the propaganda in Maharashtra was carried on in the name of Nana.

These considerations, as well as the fact that by far the greater part of India was free from any overt acts of hostility against the British Government, divest the outbreak of 1857 of a national character. We may now proceed to discuss whether it can be regarded as a war of independence. In properly judging this question we have to take into consideration the character of the outbreak as discussed above, as well as the motives of the different persons and classes who took part in it. As we have seen above, the most important elements who fought against the British were the sepoys. They had their own grievances, similar to those which led to local mutinies on many previous occasions. The utmost that can be said is that they were inspired by the motive of defending their religion against the intrigues of Christians to pollute them, and not that of regaining the freedom of their country. But even this charitable interpretation is not admitted by all. We have quoted above the opinion of Ahsanulla that the sepoys were inspired more by a desire of material gain than any political or even religious consideration. Such a view is amply supported by the conduct of the sepoys at Delhi and in other places. Far from enlisting the sympathy and support of the people at large, they were intent on plundering them and burning their villages. It is a painful but undeniable fact that both Europeans and Indians were alike victims to their fury and greed, and in many places they inspired a sense of dread and terror rather than that of sympathy and fellow-feeling among the people. The sepoys at Delhi refused to fight unless they were paid their salaries, and that on an adequate scale—a demand which is hardly in consonance with the spirit which should guide a fighter in a war of independence. Many sepoys at Delhi, Bareilly, and Allahabad, and probably in other places, too, after plundering indiscriminately, went back to their homes to enjoy the wealth they had secured, without any thought of any other question or policy. There is nothing in the conduct or behaviour of the sepoys which would justify us in the belief, or even assumption, that they were inspired by love for their country and fought against the British with the definite idea of freeing their motherland.

In this connection a very important fact is often forgotten by those who claim the outbreak of 1857 as a national war of independence, for which patriotic sepoys shed their blood, and political leaders had been preparing grounds for a long time. The Panjab was conquered by the British with the help of the sepoys less than ten years before the outbreak of Mutiny. The battle of Chillianwala which proved the valour and heroism of the Sikhs, and their ability, under more favourable circumstances, to defeat the English, was fought in 1849, only eight years before the Mutiny. If there were really a movement for freeing India from the British yoke, obviously this was the most suitable opportunity. But we have not the least evidence to show that the Indian leaders like Nana Sahib and others mentioned above raised their little finger to help the cause of the Sikhs. The sepoys themselves, who are supposed to have sacrificed their all for the sake of their country in 1857, had not the least scruple to fight the Sikhs who were the last defender of liberty in India. There are even allegations that the Sikhs entreated the sepoys to refuse help to the British, but in vain. Although this cannot be definitely proved, it should have occurred to every sepoy, who had real love for his country, that by defeating the Sikhs he would only forge the last link in the chain by which India was being fettered by the British. It is difficult to resist the conclusion that the attitude and activities of the sepoys in 1849 certainly did not correspond to the patriotic fervour with which they are supposed to be endowed in 1857. Unless, therefore, we suppose that this sentiment was suddenly developed during the short interval of eight years, we can hardly regard the sepoys, who rebelled in 1857, as being inspired by the idea of liberty and freedom. Incidentally, the Sikh War also proves the absence, in 1849, of any serious conspiracy or organisation against the British, although, according to Sitaram Bawa, such conspiracy against the British was going on for many years in almost every native court. Surely the Sikh War would have been the most suitable opportunity, if ever there were any, which the conspirators should have taken advantage of for organising a war of independence against the British.

As mentioned above, the Sikhs, along with the Gurkhas, faithfully served the British during the outbreak of 1857, and were mainly instrumental in defeating the sepoys. It is usual to blame the Sikhs for this unpatriotic act, but they could hardly be expected to pay the sepoys back other than in their own coins. The same argument also applies to the Gurkhas whose country was invaded and who were defeated by the British with the help of the sepoys in 1815.

As a matter of fact, Indian sepoys, belonging to any part of this country, never refused to fight against Indians on behalf of the British. This has been shown repeatedly in all wars of the British during the first half of the 19th century.

Nothing but the strongest positive evidence should lead us to believe that the sepoys changed almost overnight into patriotic Indians who risked their position and prospect, and even lives, merely for the sake of their country. No such evidence is, however, forthcoming. . . .

3. ANTI-BRITISH OUTBREAKS, NOT A NEW PHENOMENON

. . . The rebellion of chiefs and people in Avadh constitutes the chief claim of the outbreak of 1857 to be regarded as a war of independence. Yet we can view it in its true perspective only if we remember the numerous instances of civil resistance to the British authority. . . . If several Talukdars and other chiefs of Avadh, who took advantage of the general mutiny of British sepoys to rise against the British, are to be looked upon as fighters for independence of India, can we withhold such claim or recognition from Wazir Ali of Avadh, Pyche Raja of Malabar, Dhundia Wagh of Mysore, Lakshman Dawa of Ajaygadh, Gopal Singh of Bundelkhand, Vizieran Rauze of Vizianagram, Dhananjaya Bhanja of Gumsur, Vellu Thampi of Travancore, Jagabandhu of Khurda, the Rajas of Dhalbhum and hosts of others . . . who had the courage to rise singlehanded and defy the British authority? Even in Uttar Pradesh, Dayaram of Aligarh and Bijoy Singh of Kunja, near Rurki, opposed a greater resistance to the British authority, without any external help, than Beni Madho and others in the same province did in 1857-8. So if we regard the outbreak of 1857-8 as war of independence, we must regard such war to be in continuous operation in more extensive regions in India, almost throughout the first century of British rule. There is no special reason to select the rising of 1857-8 in U. P. as specially befitting this designation in preference to many others occurring before it.

As a matter of fact we can hardly expect a national war of independence in India either in 1857 or at any time before it. For nationalism or patriotism, in the true sense, was conspicuous by its absence in India till a much later date. To regard the outbreak of 1857 as either national in character or a war for independence of India betrays a lack of true knowledge of the history of Indian people in the nineteenth century.

The example of Syed Ahmad Khan, noted above, is of peculiar significance. He was a staunch supporter of the British during the Mutiny and yet rose to be the undisputed leader of Muslims in U. P. This proves the absence of a strong national feeling in favour of the Mutiny even within a short time of its suppression.

As a matter of fact it is clear from a perusal of contemporary literature that the Mutiny of 1857 did not evoke any sense of national feeling at the time, nor was it regarded as a national war of independence till the rise of national consciousness at the close of the nineteenth century. It is on record that public meetings were held in many parts of India condemning the Mutiny, and congratulatory addresses, even illuminations, followed notable British victories. The Sindhia fired a salute of twenty-one guns on the fall of Jhansi, and after his forced flight from Gwalior, was welcomed back to his capital by cheering crowds. Of course, we should not take all these at their face value. But taking everything into consideration it is difficult to conclude that the Mutiny was regarded at the time, or for many years afterwards, as a war of national independence.

The reasons why Indians at the beginning of the twentieth century held a different view of the Mutiny are not far to seek. The first and the foremost was, of course, the deliberate desire of the nationalist and revolutionary parties to hold up before the people a concrete example of a grim struggle for freedom against the British which might serve as a precedent and inspiration for the new generation which was about to launch a similar campaign. But even if we leave aside this or similar sentimental ground, there were also historical reasons for interpreting the Mutiny in a different light. The people of the twentieth century were so much obsessed with the idea of Pax Britannica, and so impregnated with a sense of British invincibility, that they

could not bring themselves to believe that local people or chiefs could dare or choose to rise against the authority of the Government unless there was an impelling motive or a great organisation behind it. They could not visualise the fact that half a century ago things were very different. The last embers of the anarchical conflagration, set ablaze by the fall of the Mughal Empire, had not yet died down, and during the first hundred years of British rule many local chiefs and primitive tribes did not hesitate to hurl defiance against the British authority. The chaos and anarchy in Central India were still within living memory. We have given above a detailed account of the series of civil outbreaks—some of them assuming serious proportions—that occurred during the period. It has also been shown that some of the local revolts during the Mutiny were really continuations of earlier outbreaks, the authors of which, brought under control, found an opportunity in 1857 to renew the conflict under more favourable circumstances. Save in extent of area and their simultaneous character, the popular outbreaks during the Mutiny did not differ much from those that took place during the century preceding it. Both these distinguishing characteristics are easily explained by the facility and stimulus offered by the Mutiny. The people felt, and perhaps rightly, that the whole authority of the British Government depended upon the vast force of the sepoys, and the tiny British force counted for little. They knew too little of the power of England, and recent reverses at Crimea suffered by the British at the hands of the Russians, of which very exaggerated accounts were afloat in India, made them belittle the power and might of the British Government. So when the Mutiny of sepoys took away the very prop on which the British rule in India rested, the people not unreasonably believed that their hour had come. We learn from both official and unofficial sources that the people did not raise their hands against the Government for a few days after the first outbreak of the Mutiny at Mirat and Delhi, but the inability of the British to restore their authority in Delhi and the ignominious flight of the British officers from the various stations naturally led them to believe that there was an end of the British rule in India. The tradition of the old days in the eighteenth century, when India was under free lances, had not altogether died down, and so we find a repetition on a smaller scale of what took place in Northern and Central India—the same zone that was affected in 1857—during the latter half of the eighteenth and to a certain extent, also far into the nineteenth century, in spite of the establishment of British rule. The anarchical political condition in Avadh—for it can hardly be regarded as anything else—which has been described above, faithfully reflects this state of things.

The Mutiny and Modern India

HUGH TINKER

Whatever the origins and nature of the war of 1857 may have been, there is no doubt of its enormous significance as a focus for nationalist sentiment in modern India. This aspect of the war is discussed in the following article by Hugh Tinker, a British scholar who has been particularly interested in the growth of self-government in India in the modern period. Tinker examines the results of the war on both Indian and British after 1857. He suggests that one of the general results of imperial rule everywhere in Asia, but particularly in India, was a sense of divided loyalties among the educated elite, since a man of ability and ambition who sought a career in public service had to compromise with the foreign system that dominated his country. This can be related to the failure of the educated classes to support the revolt in 1857; they saw their future bound up with the new order, as much as they might dislike it, rather than with the old rulers. Tinker also points out that because of the Mutiny the British became extremely cautious about taking any course of action that might give offence to religious susceptibilities, thus closing the door to aggressive social reform of the kind that had been foreshadowed in the 1830's. It might be argued, then, that after 1857 the Government became more sensitive to Indian opinion, and more acceptable to the groups that had political ambitions. In fact, to later nationalist leaders the attitude of the Government after 1857 seemed to be reactionary and the refusal to take the initiative in attacking social evils was, they argued, proof of its inadequacy. Another difficulty that Tinker sees in the celebration of 1857 as the beginning of the nationalist movement is its resort to violence, which stands in contradiction to the version of history that sees India's independence won through non-violence.

A society of Indian students recently invited me to talk upon what was tactfully called the events of 1857, and, as sometimes happens, my young Indian Chairman began with an excellent preliminary lecture propounding the idea that the events of 1857 constituted the first national revolt. When I said that I thought, on the whole, that the Mutiny was not an expression of nationalism, I was a little surprised to find the extremely harsh response which this induced amongst my young Indian audience; they clearly were not prepared even to consider the idea that this was not a manifestation of nationalism, and in the somewhat heated exchanges which followed one student put this question to me:

"If in 1776 the Americans had failed, would you now talk about the American Mutiny?" This was not really a very profound remark, but it scored a point, because the truth is that those of us who are historians are snobs of the worst sort: we are success snobs. If you look through almost any history you will observe that whatever succeeds is commended and whatever fails is passed over. The Chinese historians have a concept of the Mandate of Heaven: the idea that if a pretender or an invader is successful in taking over the throne, then he receives the Mandate of Heaven, and if a dynasty declines and decays, then the Mandate has been withdrawn. We are inclined to laugh at that theory, but, quite honestly, I think

From Hugh Tinker, "The Mutiny and Modern India," in *International Affairs*, vol. 34, Jan. 1958, pp. 57–65. Reprinted by permission.

we really all subscribe to the Mandate of Heaven.

The British writers who approached the Mutiny towards the end of the nineteenth century looked at it against a solid basis of British achievement in India, and to them the Mutiny was an aberration, a temporary setback to the process of building up British rule in India. But to the Indians of today the perspective looks very different. To most Indians the process of acquiring independence is seen as the result of a struggle: it follows the civil disobedience campaigns of 1920–1, 1930–1, and the risings of August 1942. It could have all been quite different: if the Indian Liberals, who at one time led the Congress, had maintained their hold, if men like Gokhale, Chintamani, or Tej Bahadur Sapru had gone on to fashion independence, the whole of Indian constitutional development would have looked rather like the consentient process in Australia or Canada or even in Ceylon. But it did not happen that way, and so most Indians regard independence as the outcome of a physical struggle against the British; and on that basis 1857 seems to form the prelude to the Nationalist Movement.

How does this relate to modern historical thought? In a recent review of the state of Asian historical studies, I put forward the view that we are all living in the "Post-Colonial Era," that, despite the coming of Independence to the former British dominions in Asia, the Colonial past still overshadows us.

Among British historians of India there are, perhaps, two schools. There are the men who have written about the British period from the point of view of former administrators, or soldiers or businessmen, whose aim, one may perhaps say, is commemorative—they write to put on record what British rule achieved in Asia. They are avowedly interpreting or justifying "Colonialism." The other sort of historians are the academics. We like to think that we are detached, but in reality we are also tied to the past. Most of us assume an attitude of apology, of uncertainty, of guilt, deriving perhaps from the influence of Edward Thompson or of J. A. Hobson. In reaction against the assured tones of nineteenth-century Imperialism we hesitate and temporize. Neither of the two schools of British historians has produced any significant reassessment of the Mutiny. The judgements made by Victorian writers have merely been reiterated or modified.

The thinking of Indian writers of the present day is also limited by preoccupation with this Colonial past. They are concerned to rehabilitate their national self-respect, as it were: to present to the world the achievements of Indian culture and to correct British assumptions regarding the period of European dominance. Two leading historians, R. C. Majumdar and Surendra Nath Sen, have just produced detailed studies of the Mutiny.[1] Both works are notable for their careful scholarship and balanced judgement. Both are based largely upon the voluminous British Mutiny literature—Kaye, Rice Holmes, Forrest, and the rest—giving their work a strangely Victorian flavour of battles and heroic deeds, very different from most of the socio-economic historical studies of the present day. Both reinforce the conventional verdicts on 1857: they reject the concept of a national war of independence (Majumdar has a section ironically headed The Heroes, in which he exposes the materialistic motives and equivocal behaviour of the leading mutineers). Both emphasize the degree of support which the British received from Indians of every class. Yet the conclusion of Majumdar is that this was "the first great and direct challenge to the British rule in India . . . [which] furnished a historical basis for the [Independence] struggle, and gave it a moral stimulus." Sen goes further and avers that "what began as a fight for religion ended as a war of independence."

Perhaps it is inevitable that Indian writers should view the recent history of

[1] For selections, see pages 84–91, and 80–83. [Editor's Note]

their country as a struggle, a clash, between Indians and foreigners. Most Indians are also concerned to look at the Mutiny in order to emphasize what seems to them important, the unity between Hindus and Muslims, which, they suggest, occurred at that time. Pakistanis, of course, have another viewpoint: they wish to write up the Mutiny as a Muslim national revolt. It is revealing to examine the manner in which the Muslims' share in the Mutiny has been handled over the years. In the 1850s, most British commentators believed in the idea of a Muslim conspiracy. Then, the writings of Sir Sayyid Ahmed and Sir William Hunter led to a view of the "loyal" Muslims; men recalled that the Muslims only constituted one out of seven of the Sepoys in the Army and their responsibility was played down. Today, in a time of Islamic revivalism, emphasis is placed by Pakistanis on the Islamic inspiration of the revolt; there has been an attempt to explore the share of the Wahabis in the origins of the Mutiny, while other Muslim writers dwell upon the spell of the old Moghul Empire over the mind of India.

Once again there is a picture of a clash between the peoples of the sub-continent and the foreigners, but I suggest that the Colonial period will, in due course, be seen as something else. It will be seen, eventually, as a partnership; its keynote, not British achievement, or Indian nationalism, but a partnership between Indians and British in Asia. This theme has been explored by Guy Wint in *The British in Asia,* but even he, I think, abandoned the idea in his second edition, with its emphasis on the triumph of Nationalism. I spend most of my time looking at South-East Asia where it is impossible to ignore the interdependence of British and Indians in every sphere, whether it be the administrative or the economic or the educational. Throughout, Indians and British are indispensable to each other and the whole of modern development moves forward as a partnership; not necessarily a willing partnership —a partnership of convenience, if you like

—but a partnership. It seems to me that this theme will eventually be recognized as paramount, and even amidst the hatred and the strife of the Mutiny it can be seen; I would like to explore the nature of this co-operation between British and Indians.

At the moment of the revolt the British troops in India were depleted, and if there had been a united rising by the Indian forces backed up by the Indian civil population then the British must have been swept into the sea. The best observers at the time, men like Herbert Edwardes, saw that quite clearly. But there was not a united Indian uprising; there remained considerable support by Indians for the British. The consequences may be seen most vividly in events in Delhi. The recapture of the city was effected by five columns, made up of 1,700 British troops and 3,200 Indians: almost twice as many. Even if the Kashmir contingent, numbering 1,200, is excluded as playing only a minor part, still, the majority of the "British" force was actually Indian. The key operation was the blowing in of the Kashmir Gate, a task accomplished by six British officers and N.C.O.s and twenty-four Indians of the Sappers and Miners. Of those twenty-four, ten were Punjabis and fourteen were men from Agra and Oudh—men with names like Ajudhia Pathak, Ram Dulari, and Tula Ram— those Brahmins and Rajputs who are supposed to have rebelled in mass rejection of British rule. In that episode one finds a microcosm of the British position in Asia: it was never wholly British, it was Indo-British, and the Empire which stretched across from Kenya to Hong Kong depended upon Indian participation all the way.

What were the motives which induced some Indians in 1857 to rise against British rule, while others fought for the British cause? Can one equate support for the rebels with patriotism and support for the British with disloyalty? Surely, the whole problem is too complex to offer any simple conclusion? Yet the British in India evolved an equally artificial concept of loyalty, if I may say so. How many times in British

India has one received a young man, coming for some minor job, with a chit from a British district official: "This man comes from a very loyal family"—meaning, of course, a family which supported the British Government. Such was the view of loyalty which was accepted quite naturally only fifteen years ago, when opposition to the British Government was given such names as disaffection or sedition. But loyalty is something much too rich to be enclosed in such categorical terms. It seems to me that, a hundred years ago, loyalty in India could not be equated with patriotism; it might well be something personal: the Sepoy had made a contract, he had eaten the Company's salt and therefore his self-respect made him keep to his bond. Or else he acknowledged caste or regimental loyalty. How often the individual Sepoy went the way the Regiment went, acquiescing in the general feeling—to stand fast, or to mutiny. But a national patriotism is very difficult to discern, and the behaviour of the different units was so often conditioned by what were completely transient factors. For instance, the Bengal Sappers and Miners at Roorkee did not join in the widespread revolts round about; they marched down from Roorkee to Meerut, and on the way they put down a number of minor outbreaks. At Meerut they began to work on entrenchments, under orders. Then, one morning, a number of British troops approached them; we are not told, but I imagine the British troops must have insulted them somehow and, suddenly, the Sappers snatched up their arms, the British troops fired at them, and these men, who had stuck steadfastly to their discipline for weeks, fled or were shot down. Time and again, that episode of the Sappers at Meerut was used by those who wanted to bring the Sepoys out: "You see: the British are only waiting, you stay by them and they will wait until the opportunity comes and then they will shoot you down."

By contrast, a completely different episode at Multan, in Skinner's Horse, which was composed very largely of men from around Delhi and Agra, of the men from the area which had supplied many of the mutineers. At Multan, they watched the Bombay regiments coming up and they became very worried. They thought that the time was coming when they would be disarmed. So some of the Indian Officers went to Major Chamberlain, their Commanding Officer, and said, "We cannot hold the men any longer. They hear it said that the British are just waiting, they are going to disarm you, and then they will seek some excuse, they will say that you rebelled and then they will shoot you all down! What can we say to the men?" Thereupon Chamberlain sent for the Regimental banker, called for a jewelled sword from the Regimental treasure chest and, handing it over to the Indian Officers, said, "You take this sword down to the men. Tell them to look after it until all this is over." And that rather theatrical gesture seems to have held the Regiment. When little things like that determined men's loyalties, how can one talk about patriotism? As one reads, increasingly, one seems to enter into an atmosphere of Greek tragedy. The Sepoys wait in their cantonments, they realize that events are moving fast; they are bewildered and it seems to them that unless they do something, they will be disarmed, and then perhaps, as they have heard, they will be shot down. And so they revolt out of sheer despair.

If one looks at the other side, at those who rallied to the British, what motives governed their actions? What does one make of the seven hundred Sepoys who stayed as part of the Lucknow Garrison? Again, one cannot really talk about patriotism. They were probably persuaded to stand firm because of the great personality of Henry Lawrence, and once they had committed themselves they were isolated from their former comrades. If they tried to desert, they were shot by the mutineers. So they stood loyally at their posts for three months, not through hope of reward, but out of a spirit of self-respect and because of the inevitability of their circumstances, their *karma*.

In the new Punjabi regiments which were raised during the Mutiny, what were their motives in siding with the British? The motives of some of them were, quite frankly, of the worst. We find Nicholson telegraphing to Edwardes at Peshawar, "I will give Mubarak Shah four hundred Horse. . . . If he is not on our side, he will be against us." Edwardes and Nicholson, quite deliberately, recruited the tribesmen and sent them down-country because they knew otherwise they would have trouble with them on the frontier. But in the greater number of the new regiments that were raised, the men enlisted because it was their traditional calling, it was their life to be soldiers; they joined for the pay, for the prestige, in some cases to get revenge on the Hindustanis; a few of them may have joined because of admiration for British leaders like Nicholson or Edwardes or Abbott; but once more "loyalty" is something that barely enters into consideration.

Amongst educated Indians at the time, again, it appears that their motives were mixed; but one does sense a definite commitment on the part of some educated Indians to this new government of the British, which they saw as an inevitable part of the development of their country, and many Indians in the Administration did actively uphold government and abhorred the Mutiny as something which could only plunge their country back into the old disorder and decay. Sayyid Ahmed upheld British district administration in Bijnor after the British officials had fled; Naini Tal, with its crowd of British refugees, was kept safe by a Brahmin official. There were many such who made a deliberate choice for British Rule, which to them meant reform and progress.

But in almost every case there must have been a divided allegiance, a complex loyalty. I do not suggest that this is peculiar to India; it seems to me that throughout the Commonwealth there is a sort of dual pull and repulsion, towards and away from Britain—affection and resentment. Sir Keith Hancock, writing about the Australian troops in the first World War, records their resentment against the "Limeys"; he talks about a "double patriotism." [1] But that, of course, is simplicity compared with India, and I suggest the only parallel is to be found in Ireland. There were instances in the first World War of Irish families where one brother was winning the M.C. in France while another brother was taking part in the Easter Rising. Both were responding to the call of loyalty as they saw it.

Amongst Indians, during the second World War, there were families in which one member fought bravely in the British-Indian Army, while another joined the Japanese "Indian National Army." One I.N.A. leader was the son of a distinguished member of the judiciary. One can imagine the complex emotional stresses that went on in that young man's mind. It seems to me that Indians or any people under Colonial rule are in an almost intolerable dilemma. If they want to work for their country, to become civil servants or soldiers or educationists, then their only course is to join the British-dominated system. Otherwise they must sacrifice the use of their talents in the way that Sri Aurobindo did when he turned his back on an I.C.S. career for a life of contemplation at Pondicherry. If they wanted to work actively for their country, then they had to embrace this foreign system, and it must have created in their minds a sense of divided loyalties, which I think still continues today and which, I suggest, is still very much part of the feeling amongst Asians, particularly in the Commonwealth. It was, and is, possible for an Indian to develop a passionate loyalty to a British institution—the Indian Civil Service, the old Indian Army, a university, the Bar—and yet to abhor British dominance. This dual response, in part an ardent adoption of British values, in part a revolt against British ascendancy, is some-

[1] W. K. Hancock, *Survey of British Commonwealth Affairs* (London, 1937), vol. i, p. 63.

thing we must attempt to understand in our relations with the new Asia.

To pass on to the consequences of the Mutiny: 1857 is usually regarded in the standard histories as the watershed to Modern India, but does this not confuse co-incidence with origin? It is true that at this time the three Universities of Calcutta, Bombay, and Madras were founded, while simultaneously the first cotton mills, the first railways, the one-anna postage all began. But these "Engines of Progress" were initiated before the Mutiny, and in my view the effect of the Mutiny was not to bring India forward into the modern world but to freeze India in the mould of 1857. During the previous quarter of a century the Government of India initiated a coherent social and political economic administrative policy. Benthamite doctrine and Evangelical belief combined to work towards political and social change. But after 1857 the Government attitude was dominated by a fear that the Mutiny should ever happen again; there was a preoccupation with religion and with the susceptibilities of the people. From that time onwards, instead of leading public opinion, the British Administration tended to act as a brake on it.

In the realm of social policy, instead of the previous steady march of reform (which had included the prohibition of Suttee, the Widow's Remarriage Act, and the so-called "Freedom of Religion" Act), after the Mutiny almost all initiative came from Indian social reformers—for example, the prohibition of child-marriage—and the result (not the result the British intended, but the result that incidentally they created) was to perpetuate the social and religious feelings which existed in 1857. The Indian States were also perpetuated in the mould of 1857. In 1841, the East India Company in Leadenhall Street had laid down a policy of "just and honourable accession of [princely] territory," and from that time onwards there was a very rapid absorption of the Indian States and an extension of the regular system of British

administration; had that policy gone on, within fifty years or so the whole of India would have become one unit. Instead, as a result of 1857 there was a complete standstill, no further annexation whatsoever; indeed, in 1881 Mysore was even returned to princely rule after fifty years under British administration. At the time this might have seemed to Indians to be a concession to the Indian point of view, but in the long run one can see that it was reactionary. The perpetuation of the princely states first of all had the effect of ruining the federal solution to India's constitutional problems in the 1930s, and, after independence, necessitated a sort of surgical operation, leaving, of course, the legacy of Kashmir.

These quite fortuitous results of the Mutiny can be summed up, I think, in the perpetuation of the spirit of communalism. This I intend to examine in the case of the Army. The Mutiny in the Bengal Army was not a consequence of caste being flouted but a result of caste being pampered, in contrast to the Madras Army where, as a condition of enlistment, all Sepoys had to mess together. But in the Bengal Army caste had been exalted and after 1857 British officers drew the conclusion that caste must be observed even more strictly. Not all of them: Edwardes, for instance, saw the error of this thinking; but in general caste or religion became ever more of an obsession with the British. So we get the creation of the caste or class companies in the Army. Each unit was sub-divided into religious groups; it was not only a division between Hindus and Muslims, but amongst the different Hindu castes, a division into Rajputs, Jats, Dogras, and so on. Then each unit had its "followers," as they were called: dhobis, bhistis, cooks, sweepers; so that the whole of the caste system was incorporated in what was supposedly a modern institution, the British-Indian Army.

The effects of this policy were to preserve religious orthodoxy. Let us just look at the Sikhs. I believe that the Army was a major factor in perpetuating the Sikhs as a separate community. Sikhism was originally a reformist creed; it was a turning away from caste. Moreover, the Sikhs are naturally enterprising, practical, business-like people: they have travelled and settled all over Asia and it is probable that in contact with the wider world they would in time have discarded their distinctive emblems, in particular the uncut hair and beard. Yet today the Sikhs are a highly integrated, class-conscious orthodox community, and I suggest this is very largely because of Army service. Because the Army enlisted only the Singhs, those who had taken the *pahul*, the ceremony of full Sikhism. Within the Army there was a differentiation between the upper and lower castes of Sikhs, between Khatri and Jat, on the one hand, and people like Lobana and Mazbi, on the other. In each Sikh unit there was a *guru* and a *granth*, and the priest and the holy book of the Sikh religion played a major part in the military attestation ceremony. We can only glance at the economic consequences of the enlistment of large numbers of Sikhs in the Army; the receipt of *Jagirs*—land grants—in the new canal colonies, the volume of pensions they received. The result of all this was to create a privileged community, which today provides a headache for the Government of India. Now I do not suggest that this kind of development was deliberate. But it was one of the incidental results of the Mutiny, and one could explore this sort of sequence in many directions, in education, for instance, or in administration.

To come to an end, let us look at the way the centenary of the Mutiny has been celebrated in India and Pakistan. You must have all observed how muted is the note with which it has been greeted, and yet I said, earlier on, that in my view Indians identify the Mutiny with the beginning of the national struggle. Why then this restrained note? There may be two reasons. The National leaders, very nobly,

do not wish to stir up racial feeling against the British. In the present difficult time, Nehru and his colleagues have quite deliberately played down the anti-British theme. But it seems to me there is another important point: they do not want to emphasize physical force. They wish to restore respect for authority, which has been sadly shaken in the last quarter of a century. In universities, schools, trade unions —in almost any sort of organization—as a result of the militant movement of pre-independence days there remains a legacy of contempt for authority. The leaders realize that this contempt for authority, encouraged during the struggle for independence, has not ceased: it has become a double-edged weapon. For this reason the cult of the I.N.A. was suddenly reversed by the Indian leaders. The example of the Mutiny, the apotheosis of violence, affords similar dangers.

What will be the final Indian verdict on the Mutiny? Historical writing in Asia today is under pressure. In some Asian countries the histories of the Freedom Movements are approached in the manner of Orwell's 1984. In the Preface to his study of the Mutiny, Professor Majumdar relates how he was constrained to withdraw from the task of compiling the "official" history because of attempts to influence his judgement, even attempts to induce him to utilize highly suspect documents. The academic tradition in India may be expected to resist crude political interference of this nature, but it may be more susceptible to the prevailing belief in non-violence.

In the present context of Indian ideas, non-violence is accepted as the essence of the Independence movement and the fierce quarter-century struggle from 1920 to 1945 is interpreted in current writing entirely in non-violent terms. Against this pattern, the Mutiny may finally assume an entirely different significance in the light of Indian thought.

SUGGESTIONS FOR ADDITIONAL READING

The bibliography of the War of 1857 is so vast that all that can be attempted in this brief note is an indication of classes of materials, with special mention being made of those books that contain fairly comprehensive listings of books and other source material. A good discussion of the general characteristics of the accounts of the War can be found in S. N. Sen's chapter on "Writings on the Mutiny" in *Historians of India, Pakistan, and Ceylon* (edited by C. H. Philips, London: 1961). Some of the general histories of modern India also have useful discussions of the historiography of 1857; the relevant chapters in Percival Spear's *India: A Modern History* (Ann Arbor: 1961), R. C. Majumdar, *et al.*, *Advanced History of India* (London: 1956), and E. J. Thompson and G. T. Garrett, *Rise and Fulfilment of British Rule in India* (London: 1934, and Allahabad: 1958) should be consulted. Since the selections and headnotes in this text are largely bibliographical in nature, the books that will be mentioned in this note are mainly source materials that have not been already cited.

Most of the official records, including despatches to and from the Government of India, reports of civil servants on the areas under their control, as well as transcripts of the trials held after the suppression of the rebellions, are available in *Parliamentary Papers*. The important volumes are as follows: 1857, vols. xxix and xxx; 1857–58, vols. xlii, xliii, and xliv; 1859, vols. xviii, xxiii, xxv, and xxxvii; 1860, vol. l; and 1863, vol. xl. Other documents may be found in Sir George Forrest's *Selections from the Letters, Despatches, and other State Papers of the Government of India,*

1857–1858 (4 vols., Calcutta: 1893–1912). Since 1947 a number of collections of documents have been made in India in an attempt to give the Indian as well as the British side of the War. Unfortunately these have not all been edited with care, but they provide some new and interesting material. The most notable of these is *Freedom Struggle in Uttar Pradesh,* edited by S. A. A. Rizvi and M. L. Bhargava (4 vols., Uttar Pradesh: 1957–59). A somewhat similar venture has been started in Pakistan entitled *A History of the Freedom Movement (being the Story of the Muslim Struggle for the Freedom of Hind-Pakistan)* (Karachi: 1957).

There are numerous contemporary accounts of the War, in addition to those excerpted in the text. These accounts may be roughly classified under four heads: letters and autobiographies of military men; diaries and letters of civilian participants; the writings of journalists and other observers; and accounts by Indians. Many of the military autobiographies were written long after the events they describe, but frequently contain letters. This is true of Lord Roberts' *Forty-One Years in India* (2 vols., London: 1924), who was a young officer in 1857 and rose to be Commander-in-chief of the Indian Army. A young lieutenant, V. D. Majendie, left a revealing account in *Up among the Pandies* (London: 1859). General Sir George Jacob's *Western India before and during the Mutinies* is a valuable book; an intelligent observer of Indian political life, he felt that changes were being made without taking into account the nature of Indian society. Biographies of the leading military figures also contain letters and other papers;

99

mention may be made of L. J. Trotter's *Life of John Nicholson* (London: 1898) and his *Bayard of India, a Study of General Sir James Outram* (Edinburgh: 1903). While these and other biographies have a hero-worshipping tone unpleasing to modern tastes, they provide much useful material.

Among the civilian officials, William Edwards, Collector at Budaun, has left two interesting accounts of his experiences: *Facts and Reflections Connected with the Indian Rebellion* (Liverpool: 1859) and *Personal Adventures during the Indian Rebellion* (London: 1858). Sir George Campbell, who had been in charge of the Cis-Satlej States, described the brutal severity used in putting down the rebellions in *Memoirs of My Indian Career* (2 vols., London: 1893). The letters of Sir John Lawrence in the *Life of Lord Lawrence* by R. B. Smith are interesting for the insight they give into the thinking of one of the ablest of the East India Company's civil servants (2 vols., London: 1883).

From non-official sources we have many letters and diaries; those of Englishwomen who lived through some of the sieges are particularly valuable as social documents indicating attitudes toward the people of India in general and the rebels in particular. Many of them have a note of ferocity absent from the writings of men like Lawrence. Mrs. Maria Germon's *Lucknow Journal* tells of the sufferings of the British during the most famous of the sieges (edited by Michael Edwardes, London: 1957). In *A Lady's Escape from Gwalior* Mrs. R. M. Coopland expresses the desire for vengeance that characterizes many of the civilian survivors (London: 1859). W. H. Russell, one of the greatest of nineteenth-century correspondents, covered the war for the London *Times*. In *My Indian Mutiny Diary* he gives a running commentary on events interspersed with his reflections of the nature of British rule in India and his disquietude because of some of the actions of his countrymen (edited by Michael Edwardes, London: 1957).

There are remarkably few contemporary Indian accounts, other than the testimonies given at trials (these may be found in *Parliamentary Papers*). Although many of the literate classes must have felt sympathy with the fate of the rebels, they were not in a position to express their feelings. One of the most famous Indians of his time, Sir Syed Ahmad Khan, did, however, discuss the nature of the war in *An Essay on the Causes of the Indian Revolt* (trans. by W. N. Lees, Calcutta: 1860). He argued that the Muslims had not been the instigators of the rebellion, as was frequently charged, but that many of them, in common with Hindus, had feared that Government and missionary activities were endangering their religion. Two other accounts by Indians are found in *Two Native Narratives of the Mutinies at Delhi* (trans. by Sir Theophilus Metcalfe, London: 1898). A recent translation, *The Memoirs of Ashanullah Khan*, provides some interesting sidelights on Indian reactions, but the text is very badly edited (Karachi: 1958).

Among general histories, the most detailed is one known as *Kaye's and Malleson's History of the Indian Mutiny* (6 vols., London: 1889–93). This is really two quite separate works; the first two volumes are by Sir John Kaye and rest are by G. B. Malleson, and available in a number of editions. Malleson must be used with caution, as he was both a tendentious and uncritical historian. T. Rice Holmes' *History of the Indian Mutiny* is a very useful summary (5th edition, London: 1913). Sir George Forrest wrote a lengthy work, *History of the Indian Mutiny*, that concentrates on the details of battles (3 vols., London: 1904–12). In many ways the best one-volume history is S. N. Sen's *Eighteen Fifty-Seven* (New Delhi: 1957). It contains a lengthy bibliography of printed source material, contemporary pamphlets, books, and journals. It should be read in conjunction with R. C. Majumdar's *The Sepoy Mutiny and Revolt of 1857*, which provides astringent criticism not only of

British historians but also of Indian historians (Calcutta: 1857).

All the works mentioned in Part III of the text will repay study in full, but they are only a small sampling of the many books and articles that have been written by Indian historians in recent years. The centenary of 1857 saw the production of many works, some of them ephemeral in nature, but almost all of some interest. The best of these may be found in the *Journal of Indian History,* particularly the issues for 1957 and 1958. Many of the books and articles by Indian historians as well as those by British and American historians are listed in the bibliographical issues of the *Journal of Asian Studies.* Volumes xvii, number 5, 1958, and xviii, number 5, 1959, should be consulted.